Poems *Deep* & Dangerous

selected by Jo Phillips

CAMBRIDGE
UNIVERSITY PRESS

PUBLISHED BY THE PRESS SYNDICATE OF THE UNIVERSITY OF CAMBRIDGE
The Pitt Building, Trumpington Street, Cambridge, United Kingdom

CAMBRIDGE UNIVERSITY PRESS
The Edinburgh Building, Cambridge CB2 2RU, UK
40 West 20th Street, New York, NY 10011–4211, USA
477 Williamstown Road, Port Melbourne, VIC 3207, Australia
Ruiz de Alarcón 13, 28014 Madrid, Spain
Dock House, The Waterfront, Cape Town 8001, South Africa

http://www.cambridge.org

First published 1995
Reprinted 2002

Printed in the United Kingdom at the University Press, Cambridge

A catalogue record for this book is available from the British Library

ISBN 0 521 47990 8

CONTENTS

1 Strictly Personal

2 Media Media

CONTENTS

4 *One Another*

5 Life and Death

Strictly personal

The Man in the Bowler Hat

I am the unnoticed, the unnoticeable man:
The man who sat on your right in the morning train:
The man you looked through like a windowpane:
The man who was the colour of the carriage, the colour of
   the mounting
Morning pipe smoke.

I am the man too busy with a living to live,
Too hurried and worried to see and smell and touch:
The man who is patient too long and obeys too much
And wishes too softly and seldom.

I am the man they call the nation's backbone,
Who am boneless – playable catgut, pliable clay:
The Man they label Little lest one day
I dare to grow.

I am the rails on which the moment passes,
The megaphone for many words and voices:
I am graph, diagram,
Composite face.

I am the led, the easily-fed,
The tool, the not-quite-fool,
The would-be-safe-and-sound,
The uncomplaining bound,
The dust fine-ground,
Stone-for-a-statue waveworn pebble-round.

A. S. J. TESSIMOND

I Am

I am – yet what I am, none cares or knows;
    My friends forsake me like a memory lost:
I am the self-consumer of my woes –
    They rise and vanish in oblivions host,
Like shadows in love frenzied stifled throes
    And yet I am, and live – like vapours tost

Into the nothingness of scorn and noise,
    Into the living sea of waking dreams,
Where there is neither sense of life nor joys,
    But the vast shipwreck of my life's esteems;
Even the dearest that I love the best
    Are strange – nay, rather, stranger than the rest.

I long for scenes where man hath never trod,
    A place where woman never smiled or wept,
There to abide with my Creator God,
    And sleep as I in childhood sweetly slept,
Untroubling and untroubled where I lie,
    The grass below, above, the vaulted sky.

JOHN CLARE

Childhood

I used to think that grown-up people chose
To have stiff backs and wrinkles round their nose,
And veins like small fat snakes on either hand,
On purpose to be grand.
Till through the banisters I watched one day
My great-aunt Etty's friend who was going away,
And how her onyx beads had come unstrung.
I saw her grope to find them as they rolled;
And then I knew she was helplessly old,
As I was helplessly young.

FRANCES CORNFORD

What Happened to the Elephant?

What happened to the elephant,
the one whose head Shiva stole
to bring his son Ganesh
        back to life?

This is the child's curiosity
the nosy imagination that continues
probing, looking for a way
to believe the fantasy
a way to prolong the story.

If Ganesh could still be Ganesh
with an elephant's head,
then couldn't the body
        of that elephant
find another life
with a horse's head – for example?

And if we found
a horse's head to revive
the elephant's body –
Who is the true elephant?
And what shall we do
about the horse's body?

Still, the child refuses
to accept Shiva's carelessness
and searches for a solution
without death.

    .   .   .   .

But now when I gaze
at the framed postcard
of Ganesh on my wall,
I also picture a rotting carcass
of a beheaded elephant
        lying crumpled up
on its side, covered with bird shit
vulture shit –

Oh that elephant
        whose head survived
for Ganesh –

He died, of course, but the others
in his herd, the hundreds
in his family must have found him.
They stared at him for hours
with their slow swaying sadness…
How they turned and turned
in a circle, with their trunks
facing outwards and then inwards
towards the headless one.

That is a dance
        a group dance
no one talks about.

SUJATA BHATT

Note: Ganesh, the son of Shiva and Parvati, is the elephant-headed god in Hindu mythology. He is a symbol
for wisdom and prudence. It is important to note that Ganesh did not always have an elephant's head, but
acquired one after Shiva through a misunderstanding chopped off his original (human) head.

Children's Song

We live in our own world,
A world that is too small
For you to stoop and enter
Even on hands and knees,
The adult subterfuge.
And though you probe and pry
With analytic eye,
And eavesdrop all our talk
With an amused look,
You cannot find the centre
Where we dance, where we play,
Where life is still asleep
Under the closed flower,
Under the smooth shell
Of eggs in the cupped nest
That mock the faded blue
Of your remoter heaven.

R. S. THOMAS

Nativity Play

(the angel speaks)

– what gets me
is putting on some girl's negligé

with the wire frame of the wings
jabbing my back

– as for the halo
it's just a ring of neon

rigged up by the science master,
to switch on under my nightie.

Who invented angels anyway?
Miss says things about being ethereal

and a revelation and all that.
I don't believe in angels –

they're something dreamed up
to populate heaven, and as for flying,

I've too much earthly weight
to rise off the ground.

I only said I'd do it to get off games.

TILLA BRADING

A Far Cry from Africa

A wind is ruffling the tawny pelt
Of Africa. Kikuyu, quick as flies,
Batten upon the bloodstreams of the veldt.
Corpses are scattered through a paradise.
Only the worm, colonel of carrion, cries:
'Waste no compassion on these separate dead!'
Statistics justify and scholars seize
The salients of colonial policy.
What is that to the white child hacked in bed?
To savages, expendable as Jews?

Threshed out by beaters, the long rushes break
In a white dust of ibises whose cries
Have wheeled since civilization's dawn
From the parched river or beast-teeming plain.
The violence of beast on beast is read
As natural law, but upright man
Seeks his divinity by inflicting pain.
Delirious as these worried beasts, his wars
Dance to the tightened carcass of a drum,
While he calls courage still that native dread
Of the white peace contracted by the dead.

Again brutish necessity wipes its hands
Upon the napkin of a dirty cause, again
A waste of our compassion, as with Spain,
The gorilla wrestles with the superman.
I who am poisoned with the blood of both,
Where shall I turn, divided to the vein?
I who have cursed
The drunken officer of British rule, how choose
Between this Africa and the English tongue I love?
Betray them both, or give back what they give?
How can I face such slaughter and be cool?
How can I turn from Africa and live?

DEREK WALCOTT

The Centre of the Universe

i   Pushing my trolley about in the supermarket,
I am the centre of the universe;
Up and down the aisles of beans and juices,
I am the centre of the universe;
It does not matter that I live alone;
It does not matter that I am a jilted lover;
It does not matter that I am a misfit in my job;
I am the centre of the universe.

But I'm always here, if you want me –
For I am the centre of the universe.

ii   I enjoy being the centre of the universe.
It is not easy being the centre of the universe
But I enjoy it.
I take pleasure in,
I delight in,
Being the centre of the universe.
At six o'clock a.m. this morning I had a phone call;
It was from a friend, a man in Los Angeles:
'Paul, I don't know what time it is in Dublin
But I simply had to call you:
I cannot stand LA so I thought I'd call you.'
I calmed him down as best I could.

I'm always here, if you want me –
For I am the centre of the universe.

iii   I had barely put the phone down when it rang again,
This time from a friend in São Paulo in Brazil:
'Paul – do you know what is the population of São Paulo?
I will tell you: it is twelve million skulls.
Twelve million pairs of feet in the one footbath.
Twelve million pairs of eyes in the one fishbowl.
It is unspeakable, I tell you, unspeakable.'
I calmed him down.

I'm always here, if you want me –
For I am the centre of the universe.

iv   But then when the phone rang a third time and it was not
      yet 6.30 a.m.,
The petals of my own hysteria began to wake up and unfurl.
This time it was a woman I know in New York City:
'Paul – New York City is a Cage',
And she began to cry a little bit over the phone,
To sob over the phone,
And from five thousand miles away I mopped up her tears.
I dabbed each tear from her cheek
With just a word or two or three from my calm voice.

I'm always here, if you want me –
For I am the centre of the universe.

v   But now tonight it is myself;
Sitting at my aluminium double-glazed window in Dublin city;
Crying just a little bit into my black tee shirt.
If only there was just one human being out there
With whom I could make a home? Share a home?
Just one creature out there in the night –
Is there not just one creature out there in the night?
In Helsinki, perhaps? Or in Reykjavik?
Or in Chapelizod? Or in Malahide?
So you see, I have to calm myself down also
If I am to remain the centre of the universe;
It's by no means an exclusively self-centred automatic thing
Being the centre of the universe.

I'm always here, if you want me –
For I am the centre of the universe.

PAUL DURCAN

Telephone Conversation

The price seemed reasonable, location
Indifferent. The landlady swore she lived
Off premises. Nothing remained
But self-confession. 'Madam, ' I warned,
'I hate a wasted journey – I am African. '
Silence. Silenced transmission of
Pressurised good-breeding. Voice, when it came,
Lipstick coated, long gold-rolled
Cigarette-holder pipped. Caught I was, foully.
'HOW DARK?'... I had not misheard... 'ARE YOU LIGHT
OR VERY DARK?' Button B. Button A. Stench
Of rancid breath of public hide-and-speak.
Red booth. Red pillar-box. Red double-tiered
Omnibus squelching tar. It *was* real! Shamed
By ill-mannered silence, surrender
Pushed dumbfoundment to beg simplification.
Considerate she was, varying the emphasis –
'ARE YOU DARK? OR VERY LIGHT?' Revelation came.
'You mean – like plain or milk chocolate?'
Her assent was clinical, crushing in its light
Impersonality. Rapidly, wave-length adjusted,
I chose. 'West African sepia'– and as afterthought,
'Down in my passport.' Silence for spectroscopic
Flight of fancy, till truthfulness clanged her accent
Hard on the mouthpiece. 'WHAT'S THAT?' conceding
'DON'T KNOW WHAT THAT IS.' 'Like brunette.'
'THAT'S DARK ISN'T IT?' 'Not altogether.
Facially, I am brunette, but, madam, you should see
The rest of me. Palm of my hand, soles of my feet
Are a peroxide blond. Friction, caused –
Foolishly, madam – by sitting down, has turned
My bottom raven black – One moment, madam!' – sensing
Her receiver rearing on the thunderclap
About my ears – 'Madam, ' I pleaded, 'wouldn't you rather
See for yourself?'

WOLE SOYINKA

Campsite: Maentwrog

This field contains the modest apparatus
Of suburb life, incubating under
Separate bell-jars, hurricane lamp-lit.

We observe it. Domesticated mum
In the permanent apron, and dad, reverting
In the wild to a feral state,

Shirt-sleeved, morose. The quarrelling lovers
Rained on, in the car, by dashboard-light.
He pitched the tent alone; they left at dawn.

Children fetching milk and water, making
Work a ritual, like games, and playing
Only with children from respectable tents.

The flat-capped fisherman, working his punctual
Day-shift on the river, whose dog
Knew to expect him at tea-time. And you

And me, patrolling the domestic purlieus,
Getting on with knitting and letters,
All of us practising our characteristic selves,

Despite the grass, and the apologetically
Insistent rain. Abroad we should be
Other, conforming to the strangeness

Of bread and air. Here we are just
Ourselves forced under glass. You have to pay more
For expensive weather. This is a cheap country.

U. A. FANTHORPE

At Least a Hundred Words

What shall we say in our letters home?
That we're perfectly all right?
That we stand on the playground with red faces
and our hair sticking up?
That we give people Chinese burns?
Mr Ray, standing in the entrance to the lavatories
with his clip-board and pen,
turned us round by our heads
and gave us a boot up the arse.
We can't put that in our letters home
because Mr Ray is taking letter-writing.
He sits in his master's chair
winding the propeller of his balsa wood aeroplane
with a glue-caked index finger
and looking straight ahead.
RESULTS OF THE MATCH, DESCRIPTION OF THE FLOODS,
THE LECTURE ON KENYA, UGANDA AND TANGANYIKA
WITH COLOUR SLIDES AND HEADDRESSES.
We have to write at least a hundred words
to the satisfaction of Mr Ray
before we can go in to tea,
so I put up my hand to ask if we count the 'ands'.
Mr Ray lets go the propeller of his Prestwick 'Pioneer'
and it unwinds with a long drawn-out sigh.
He'd rather be out overflying
enemy territory on remote
than 'ministering to the natives' in backward C4.
He was shot down in World War One or World War
Two, he forgets,
but it didn't do him a damn bit of harm.
It made a man of him.
He goes and stands in the corner near the door
and offers up his usual prayer:
'One two three four five six seven
God give me strength to carry on.'
While his back is turned
I roll a marble along the groove in the top of my desk
till it drops through the inkwell

on to the track I've made for it inside. I can hear it
travelling round the system of books
and rulers: a tip-balance, then a spiral,
then a thirty-year gap as it falls through
the dust-hole into my waiting hand.

HUGO WILLIAMS

One

Only one of me
and nobody can get a second one
from a photocopy machine.

Nobody has the fingerprints I have.
Nobody can cry my tears, or laugh my laugh
or have my expectancy when I wait.

But anybody can mimic my dance with my dog.
Anybody can howl how I sing out of tune.
And mirrors can show me multiplied
many times, say, dressed up in red
or dressed up in grey.

Nobody can get into my clothes for me
or feel my fall for me, or do my running.
Nobody hears my music for me, either.

I am just this one.
Nobody else makes the words
I shape with sound, when I talk.

But anybody can act how I stutter in a rage.
Anybody can copy echoes I make.
And mirrors can show me multiplied
many times, say, dressed up in green
or dressed up in blue.

JAMES BERRY

Childhood of a Voice

The light oppresses and the darkness frees
a man like me, who never cared at all:
Imagine it, the childhood of a voice
and voice of childhood telling me my name.

But if only the rain would fall,
and the sky we have not seen so long
come blue again.

The familiar white street
is tired of always running east.
The sky, of always arching over.
The tree, of always reaching up.

Even the round earth is tired of being round
and spinning round the sun.

MARTIN CARTER

From Keats' *Ode to Sorrow*

... To Sorrow,
    I bade good-morrow,
And thought to leave her far away behind;
    But cheerly, cheerly,
    She loves me dearly;
She is so constant to me, and so kind:
    I would deceive her,
    And so leave her,
But ah! she is so constant and so kind.

Beneath my palm trees, by the river side,
I sat a weeping: in the whole world wide
There was no one to ask me why I wept;
    And so I kept
Brimming the water-lily cups with tears
    Cold as my fears.

JOHN KEATS

Embankment at Night, Before the War

Charity

> By the river
> In the black wet night as the furtive rain slinks down,
> Dropping and starting from sleep
> Alone on a seat
> A woman crouches.
>
> I must go back to her.
>
> I want to give her
> Some money. Her hand slips out of the breast of her gown
> Asleep. My fingers creep
> Carefully over the sweet
> Thumb-mound, into the palm's deep pouches.
>
> So, the gift!
>
> God, how she starts!
> And looks at me, and looks in the palm of her hand!
> And again at me!
> I turn and run
> Down the Embankment, run for my life.
>
> But why? – why?
>
> Because of my heart's
> Beating like sobs, I come to myself, and stand
> In the street spilled over splendidly
> With wet, flat lights. What I've done
> I know not, my soul is in strife.
>
> The touch was on the quick. I want to forget.

D. H. LAWRENCE

Sheltered Garden

I have had enough.
I gasp for breath.

Every way ends, every road,
every foot-path leads at last
to the hill-crest –
then you retrace your steps,
or find the same slope on the other side,
precipitate.

I have had enough –
border-pinks, clove-pinks, wax-lilies,
herbs, sweet-cress.

O for some sharp swish of a branch –
there is no scent of resin
in this place,
no taste of bark, of coarse weeds,
aromatic, astringent –
only border on border of scented pinks.

Have you seen fruit under cover
that wanted light –
pears wadded in cloth,
protected from the frost,
melons, almost ripe,
smothered in straw?

H. D.

The Student

I am quilt ridden
My work unstarted
My paper blank
I have been using opium ink again.

Outside the blossom telescopes into fruit,
Inside my mind there is a blight.
A train whistles
I reshelve my books,
Shunting them into another sidetrack.
I don't feel up to it today,
Tomorrow I'll get down to it.

The party will be good experience,
There's bound to be a discussion.
I'll work all night tonight,
Tomorrow I'll work all day.

The commercial whirlpool
Draws me into town.
I buy some study aids,
They will act as pacemakers.
I rearrange my furniture,
Now the stadium is set for action.
Meanwhile my grant is being gobbled up
By that scythe-armed bandit,
'Jack Pot or Not?'

DEREK POWER

Bogyman

Stepping down from the blackberry bushes
he stands in my path: Bogyman.
He is not as I had remembered him,
though he still wears the broad-brimmed hat,
the rubber-soled shoes and the woollen gloves.
No face; and that soft mooning voice
still spinning its endless distracting yarn.

But this is daylight, a misty autumn
Sunday, not unpopulated
by birds. I can see him in such colours
as he wears – fawn, grey, murky blue –
not all shadow-clothed, as he was that night
when I was ten; he seems less tall
(I have grown) and less muffled in silence.

I have no doubt at all, though, that he is
Bogyman. He is why children
do not sleep all night in their tree-houses.
He is why, when I had pleaded
to spend a night on the common, under
a cosy bush, and my mother
surprisingly said yes, she took no risk.

He was the risk I would not take: better
to make excuses, to lose face,
than to meet the really faceless, the one
whose name was too childish for us
to utter – 'murderers' we talked of, and
'lunatics escaped from Earlswood'.
But I met him, of course, as we all do.

Well, that was then; I survived; and later
survived meetings with his other
forms, bold or pathetic or disguised – the
slummocking figure in a dark
alley, or the lover turned suddenly
icy-faced; fingers at my throat
and ludicrous violence in kitchens.

I am older now, and (I tell myself,
circling carefully around him
at the far edge of the path, pretending
I am not in fact confronted)
can deal with such things. But what, Bogyman,
shall I be at twice my age? (At
your age?) Shall I be grandmotherly, fond

suddenly of gardening, chatty with
neighbours? Or strained, not giving in,
writing for *Ambit* and hitch-hiking to
Turkey? Or sipping Guinness in
the Bald-Faced Stag, in wrinkled stockings? Or
(and now I look for the first time
straight at you) something like you, Bogyman?

FLEUR ADCOCK

Crab

Late at night we wrench open a crab;
flesh bursts out of its cup

in pastel colours. The dark fronds attract me:
Poison, you say, Dead Men's Fingers –

don't put them in your mouth, stop!
They brush over my tongue, limp and mossy,

until you snatch them from me, as you snatch
yourself, gently, if I come too close.

Here are the permitted parts of the crab,
wholesome on their nests of lettuce

and we are safe again in words.
All day the kitchen will smell of sea.

FLEUR ADCOCK

La Belle Dame sans Merci

'O what can ail thee, knight-at-arms,
  Alone and palely loitering?
The sedge is wither'd from the lake,
  And no birds sing.

'O what can ail thee, knight-at-arms,
  So haggard and so woe-begone?
The squirrel's granary is full,
  And the harvest's done.

'I see a lily on thy brow
  With anguish moist and fever dew;
And on thy cheek a fading rose
  Fast withereth too.'

'I met a lady in the meads,
  Full beautiful – a faery's child,
Her hair was long, her foot was light,
  And her eyes were wild.

'I made a garland for her head,
  And bracelets too, and fragrant zone;
She look'd at me as she did love,
  And made sweet moan.

'I set her on my pacing steed
  And nothing else saw all day long,
For sideways would she lean, and sing
  A faery's song.

'She found me roots of relish sweet,
  And honey wild and manna dew,
And sure in language strange she said,
  "I love thee true!"

'She took me to her elfin grot,
  And there she wept and sigh'd full sore;
And there I shut her wild, wild eyes
  With kisses four.

'And there she lullèd me asleep,
    And there I dream'd – Ah! woe betide!
The latest dream I ever dream'd
    On the cold hill's side.

'I saw pale kings and princes too,
    Pale warriors, death-pale were they all;
Who cried – "La belle Dame sans Merci
    Hath thee in thrall!"

'I saw their starved lips in the gloam
    With horrid warning gapèd wide,
And I awoke and found me here
    On the cold hill's side.

'And this is why I sojourn here
    Alone and palely loitering,
Though the sedge is wither'd from the lake,
    And no birds sing.'

JOHN KEATS

Sorrow

Why does the thin grey strand
Floating up from the forgotten
Cigarette between my fingers,
Why does it trouble me?

Ah, you will understand:
When I carried my mother downstairs,
A few times only, at the beginning
Of her soft-footed malady,

I should find, for a reprimand
To my gaiety, a few long grey hairs
On the breast of my coat; and one by one
I watched them float up the dark chimney.

D. H. LAWRENCE

Balloons

Since Christmas they have lived with us,
Guileless and clear,
Oval soul-animals,
Taking up half the space,
Moving and rubbing on the silk

Invisible air drifts,
Giving a shriek and pop
When attacked, then scooting to rest, barely trembling.
Yellow cathead, blue fish –
Such queer moons we live with

Instead of dead furniture!
Straw mats, white walls
And these travelling
Globes of thin air, red, green,
Delighting

The heart like wishes or free
Peacocks blessing
Old ground with a feather
Beaten in starry metals.
Your small

Brother is making
His balloon squeak like a cat.
Seeming to see
A funny pink world he might eat on the other side of it,
He bites,
Then sits
Back, fat jug
Contemplating a world clear as water.
A red
Shred in his little fist.

SYLVIA PLATH

An Irish Airman Foresees his Death

I know that I shall meet my fate
Somewhere among the clouds above;
Those that I fight I do not hate,
Those that I guard I do not love;
My country is Kiltartan Cross,
My countrymen Kiltartan's poor,
No likely end could bring them loss
Or leave them happier than before.
Nor law, nor duty bade me fight,
Nor public men, nor cheering crowds,
A lonely impulse of delight
Drove to this tumult in the clouds;
I balanced all, brought all to mind,
The years to come seemed waste of breath.
A waste of breath the years behind
In balance with this life, this death.

W. B. YEATS

Under the Stairs

Look in the dark alcove under the stairs:
a paintbrush steeped in turpentine, its hairs

softening for use; rat-poison in a jar;
bent spoons for prising lids; a spare fire-bar;

the shaft of a broom; a tyre; assorted nails;
a store of candles for when the light fails.

FRANK ORMSBY

To Make a Prairie

To make a prairie it takes a clover and one bee,
One clover, and a bee,
And revery.
The revery alone will do,
If bees are few.

EMILY DICKINSON

Children Imagining a Hospital

for Kingswood County Primary School

I would like kindness, assurance,
A wide selection of books;
Lots of visitors, and a friend
To come and see me:
A bed by the window so I could look at
All the trees and fields, where I could go for
      a walk.
I'd like a hospital with popcorn to eat.
A place where I have my own way.

I would like HTV all to myself
And people bringing tea round on trollies;
Plenty of presents and plenty of cards
(I would like presents of food).
Things on the walls, like pictures, and things
That hang from the ceiling;
Long corridors to whizz down in wheelchairs.
Not to be left alone.

U. A. FANTHORPE

Media *Media*

The Projectionist's Nightmare

This is the projectionist's nightmare:
A bird finds its way into the cinema,
finds the beam, flies down it,
smashes into a screen depicting a garden,
a sunset and two people being nice to each other.
Real blood, real intestines, slither down
the likeness of a tree.
'This is no good,' screams the audience,
'This is not what we came to see.'

BRIAN PATTEN

Writing a Letter

With what colours will I daub
the meaning of these words? I hesitate over
the palette of everything, wondering
which is the gayest, which is on the point
of exploding with joy.

And gray, the shy one, tries
not to be noticed. It bows its head,
smiling quietly to itself. Already it knows
I'll brush it, so gently,
over my gaudy meanings. They'll come to you
like a little girl in a plain frock
coming to tea. Knees together, hands in her lap,
she'll say *Please,* and I'll wait anxiously
for the small voice also to say *Thank you.*

NORMAN MacCAIG

Essential Beauty

In frames as large as rooms that face all ways
And block the ends of streets with giant loaves,
Screen graves with custard, cover slums with praise
Of motor-oil and cuts of salmon, shine
Perpetually these sharply-pictured groves
Of how life should be. High above the gutter
A silver knife sinks into golden butter,
A glass of milk stands in a meadow, and
Well-balanced families, in fine
Midsummer weather, owe their smiles, their cars,
Even their youth, to that small cube each hand
Stretches towards. These, and the deep armchairs
Aligned to cups at bedtime, radiant bars
(Gas or electric), quarter-profile cats
By slippers on warm mats,
Reflect none of the rained-on streets and squares.

They dominate outdoors. Rather, they rise
Serenely to proclaim pure crust, pure foam,
Pure coldness to our live imperfect eyes
That stare beyond this world, where nothing's made
As new or washed quite clean, seeking the home
All such inhabit. There, dark-raftered pubs
Are filled with white-clothed ones from tennis-clubs,
And the boy puking his heart out in the Gents
Just missed them, as the pensioner paid
A halfpenny more for Granny Graveclothes' Tea
To taste old age, and dying smokers sense
Walking towards them through some dappled park
As if on water that unfocused she
No match lit up, nor drag ever brought near,
Who now stands newly clear,
Smiling, and recognising, and going dark.

PHILIP LARKIN

This Poem ...

This poem is dangerous: it should not be left
Within the reach of children, or even of adults
Who might swallow it whole, with possibly
Undesirable side-effects. If you come across
An unattended, unidentified poem
In a public place, do not attempt to tackle it
Yourself. Send it (preferably, in a sealed container)
To the nearest centre of learning, where it will be rendered
Harmless, by experts. Even the simplest poem
May destroy your immunity to human emotions.
All poems must carry a Government warning. Words
Can seriously affect your heart.

ELMA MITCHELL

Sadness as Billy's Leeks Fail to Win
a Posthumous Prize

PE teacher weds rugby player.
Cat vendetta, claims owner.
Police saw man in ski mask run from store.
Pair went too far. Youth swore.

Rottweiler killed goat. Car ran into horse.
Hanging baskets repaired. New bins sought.
Tools taken. Bucket stolen.
Car wrecks goal posts. Car wasn't stolen.

Beer bottle hit car. Tax disc out of date.
Landlady is fined for pub's slate.
Karaoke complaints. House could be school.
Cow falls into swimming pool.

Firemen start fire. Vicar joins sewage gang.
Angry man broke window of caravan.
Library under attack. Police van stoned.
More police wanted. Enough post boxes.

LINDA FRANCE

Penal Servitude for Mrs Maybrick

She will not have to climb golden stairs

The Maybrick trial is over now, there's been a lot of jaw,
    Of doctors' contradiction, and expounding of the law;
She had Sir Charles Russell to defend her as we know,
    But tho' he tried his very best it all turned out no go.

Chorus
    But Mrs Maybrick will not have to climb the golden stairs;
Tho' the Jury's found her guilty and she nearly said her prayers;
She's at another kind of mashing and at it she must stop,
    Old Berry he's took down a peg with his big long drop.

Now at the trial the doctors had a very gay old time,
    They all told different stories about this cruel crime;
Some said that Mr Maybrick to death had dosed himself,
    While others said it was his wife that put him on the shelf.

Then came the servants' story how the flypapers were found,
    In fact it seems the missis had arsenic all around,
In food and drink of every kind, in cupboard and in box,
    In handkerchiefs, and even in the pockets of her frocks.

Next came the waiter's story about her trip to town,
    Which proved that from the virtue of a wife she had fell down,
And when a woman like her from her husband goes astray,
    It plainly shows she wishes that he was out of the way.

Then came the fatal letter that fairly cooked her goose,
    It seemed to say to Brierly that she soon meant to be loose;
And tho' she made a statement to explain it all away,
    The Jury wouldn't have it, you are guilty they did say.

Then to each gay and flighty wife may this a warning be,
    Don't write to any other man or sit upon his knee;
When once you start like Mrs Maybrick perhaps you couldn't stop,
    So stick close to your husband and keep clear of Berry's drop.

ANON

Victorian broadsheet in Bodleian Library, Oxford. Murder committed 1889.

In the Desert Knowing Nothing

Here I am in the desert knowing nothing,
here I am knowing nothing
in the desert of knowing nothing,
here I am in this wide
desert long after midnight.

here I am knowing nothing
hearing the noise of the rain
and the melt of fat in the pan

here is our man on the phone knowing something
and here's our man fresh from the briefing
in combat jeans and a clip microphone
testing for sound,
catching the desert rain, knowing something,

here's the general who's good with his men
storming the camera, knowing something
in the pit of his Americanness
here's the general taut in his battledress
and knowing something

Here's the boy washing his kit in a tarpaulin
on a front-line he knows from his GCSE
coursework on Wilfred Owen
and knowing something

here is the plane banking,
the *go go go* of the adrenalin
the child melting
and here's the grass that grows overnight
from the desert rain, feeling for him
and knowing everything

and here I am knowing nothing
in the desert of knowing nothing
dry from not speaking.

HELEN DUNMORE

The Film of God

Sound, too? The recorder
that picks up everything picked
up nothing but the natural
background. What language
does the god speak? And the camera's
lens, as sensitive to
an absence as to a presence,
saw what? What is the colour
of his thought?
                    It was blank, then,
the screen, as far as he
was concerned? It was a bare
landscape and harsh, and geological
its time. But the rock was
bright, the illuminated manuscript
of the lichen. And a shadow,
as we watched, fell, as though
of an unseen writer bending over
his work.
                    It was not cloud
because it was not cold,
and dark only from the candlepower
behind it. And we waited
for it to move, silently
as the spool turned, waited
for the figure that cast it
to come into view for us to
identify it, and it
didn't and we are still waiting.

R. S. THOMAS

Computer Dating

I saw you as a neutral stranger,
shut away, blinds drawn,
but you've become me, part of me,
with my passions and ideas
scrawled across your face.

Sometimes you withhold from me
and I rage and threaten,
asking more from you
than you can give:
I turn my back on you
and switch off.

Now on better terms
we'll make a compromise:
I'll not try and rush you,
go leaping ahead
but will follow instructions
to the dot …

And you'll allow me
to scroll back pages,
review and ponder
electric encounters,
rewrite our story
in Brackets and **Bold.**

JO PHILLIPS

Pavement Artist

This has always been a vanishing occupation.
In Winter he kneels to The Old Masters,
At Christmas to The Nativity.

He suffers the longest overcoat
Murky with colour,
Half-mittens, scarf and balaclava.
His chalks fester in a battered biscuit tin,
On the ground an ancient collecting cap,
The best of his art.

Summer is always sentimental,
Horses, animals, children,
The beach at Brighton.
A conveyor belt of pictures
Each one stopped in the perfect still
Of the pavement video.

He lives entirely for the present.
After the rain we discover
Faded fragments like medieval frescos
To puzzle over.

DEREK POWER

Engineers' Corner

Why isn't there an Engineers' Corner in Westminster Abbey? In Britain we've always made more fuss of a ballad than a blueprint … How many schoolchildren dream of becoming great engineers?

Advertisement placed in The Times *by the Engineering Council*

We make more fuss of ballads than of blueprints –
That's why so many poets end up rich,
While engineers scrape by in cheerless garrets.
Who needs a bridge or dam? Who needs a ditch?

Whereas the person who can write a sonnet
Has got it made. It's always been the way,
For everybody knows that we need poems
And everybody reads them every day.

Yes, life is hard if you choose engineering –
You're sure to need another job as well;
You'll have to plan your projects in the evenings
Instead of going out. It must be hell.

While well-heeled poets ride around in Daimlers,
You'll burn the midnight oil to earn a crust,
With no hope of a statue in the Abbey,
With no hope, even, of a modest bust.

No wonder small boys dream of writing couplets
And spurn the bike, the lorry and the train.
There's far too much encouragement for poets –
That's why this country's going down the drain.

WENDY COPE

Poetical Neighbour

What is it about the moon
that so utterly fascinates him,
standing out there on the lawn at night
white naked to the waist?
From my window it's just a saucer
of congealing milk,
an acne riddled rump
or discarded toenail.
Nothing very fascinating at all.
But there he is, moon blinded,
the archetypal lunatic
on about the light that calms us,
the heavenly orb.

'Oy, it's just a lump of stone,
now get off my lawn.'

He looks my way and smiles,
turns towards his home,
but pauses …
Oh God, he's seen the bloody daffodils.

JOHN HAWKHEAD

The Cat and the Boot

Or, an Improvement upon Mirrors

As I one morning shaving sat,
   For dinner-time preparing,
A dreadful howling from the cat
   Set all the room a staring!
Suddenly I turn'd – beheld a scene
   I could not but delight in;
For in my boots, so bright and clean,
   The Cat her face was fighting.
Bright was the boot – its surface fair,
   In lustre nothing lacking;
I never saw one half so clear,
   Except by WARREN's *Blacking*.
(WARREN! that name shall last as long
   As beaux and belles shall dash on,
Immortalis'd in every song
   That chaunts the praise of fashion.
For oh! without his *Blacking,* all
   Attempts we may abolish
To raise upon our boots at all
   The least of jet or polish.)
Surpris'd, its brilliancy I view'd
   With silent admiration;
The glass that on the table stood
   Wax'd dimly in its station.
I took the Boot, the glass displac'd,
   For soon I was aware,
The latter only was disgrac'd
   Whene'er the Boot was near.
And quickly found that I could shave
   Much better by its bloom,
Than any mirror that I have
   Within my drawing-room.
And since that time, I've often smil'd
   To think how puss was frighten'd.
When at the Boot she tugg'd and toil'd,
   By WARREN's *Blacking* brighten'd.

ANON

Advertisement, early nineteenth century.

Snapshotland

In Snapshotland everyone is happy all the time.
It is the promised land where people sit with flasks of tea
on smooth sand by a flat sea and smile and smile and smile.

The sun shines all day long and every day in Kodachrome
or sepia on sandboys and sandgirls who never
stop smiling from the time they first appear, with buckets,
in crisp, gingham pinafores and bonnets on the sea-shore.

Lovers stay in love forever; married couples never
grow tired of each other; everything is always just right.
The dolphins know exactly when to leap into the air
and stay there for the permanent delight of passengers
abroad the pleasure-boat which never passes out of sight.

Nobody in Snapshotland grows old unless they want to,
judging by the way they go on smiling so, in deck-chairs,
on the beach, or in old-fashioned gardens with lavender
and grandchildren here and there – and no-one dies, ever.

Even if they don't appear later, the people are still
always there, smiling through the lavender and dolphins
and the buckets full of pebbles on the same sea-shore.

SYLVIA KANTARIS

Background Material

My writing desk. Two photos, mam and dad.
A birthday, him. Their ruby wedding, her.
Neither one a couple and both bad.
I make out what's behind them from the blur.

Dad's in our favourite pub, now gone for good.
My father and his background are both gone,
but hers has my Welsh cottage and a wood
that still shows those same greens eight summers on,
though only the greenness of it's stayed the same.

Though one of them's in colour and one's not,
the two are joined, apart from their shared frame,
by what, for photographers, would mar each shot:

in his, if you look close, the gleam, the light,
me in his blind right eye, but minute size —

in hers, as though just cast from where I write,
a shadow holding something to its eyes.

TONY HARRISON

Six Schoolgirls

I met them for half a day
(we were making a TV programme)
in my familiar room. We talked
about poetry and were taken out
for an extravagant lunch. Such ice-cream!

I've thought of them since
with such relish of their likenesses
and differences it adds up
to affection.
It'll be strange when the TV flickers
and steadies and there they are, successfully
hiding their shyness.

Will I recognise in them
(so composed, so informed, so subtle)
those gossiping youngsters devouring
such soups and steaks? Such ice-cream?

NORMAN MacCAIG

Advertisement

The codfish lays a million eggs,
The helpful hen lays one.
The codfish makes no fuss of its achievement.
The hen boasts what she's done.
We forget the gentle codfish,
The hen we eulogise:
Which teaches us this lesson that –
It pays to advertise!

ANON

The Old Story

Too late to unsay what grows into speech.
Too late to refuse the rivers and creeper
unwinding from feet. Our parts have been played
by witch and trickster, knight and maid.
Troubadours have sung us, novels allowed us
adulteries. We've been christened in anthologies.

So let us beware old treacheries –
leave the liege and his lady at the stile,
her hand in his, and beg them go
no further. What would they do with rings
and lockets, troths and trysts in counties
where brothels replace bowers, and sweetness

is lost in the sprawl of affluent immoralities?
I would rather be long ago with you –
before breath was centrally heated, when sonnets
believed in people like us and needing
and owning were honest weaknesses not fought
neurotically. Just think. We could have ridden

in a carriage as in a secret, proud outcasts
of conformity. But instead of harness bells,
I hear the sages nagging me to drop
the blood's reliquaries and not convert into day
my dreams of you whom I miss like a home.
I cannot manage yet to withdraw

from our alehouses and treasuries. And rather
than exploit rhythms in your ageless company,
I'll watch with you the liege and his lady
talking analytically in modern idioms
as, with exactly the same inheritance,
they stroll inevitably through us to doom.

PATRICIA McCARTHY

My Family

Did you see us on the telly, Mum?
When we sailed away
Laughing, waving, cheering
Like in films of yesterday.

Did you read it in *The Sun,* Pop?
How we pasted them first time.
You told me all about your war.
What do you think of mine?

Did you get the letters home, dear?
How I missed you and was sad.
Did you give my love to Tracy?
Does she miss her funny Dad?

Did you see us on the hillside?
Could you spot which one was me?
Were the flowers very heavy
For a grown up girl of three?

PAUL D. WAPSHOTT

Family Portraits

1 Photograph by Herbert Tear, 12 Clapham Road, London SW

An oval frame
for the ovals of face and ears.
Smooth puff of hair
swept from the calm forehead.
Full gathers of blouse
spreading from the yoke.
The nose curls firmly, the strong chin is cleft.
Lips full, mouth slightly open,
white teeth rest on the lower lip.

Her gaze is direct, her brows level,
yet the eyes betray an asymmetry
which the high lace collar, the gold
watch on its light chain
cannot contain. It is a child's face,
plump, sensuous, awaiting experience;
naked over the soft fabric,
a brooch pinned through at her throat.

She was a servant
in a big house, running up and downstairs,
hoping for letters from her distant family,
scribbling verses in an exercise book,
writing to her father in doggerel rhymes,
jotting down songs from music halls,
sketching her own rough drawings
at the ends of the watercolour books
her employers' children threw away.
Soon he would come, the sailor lover,
and take her to the strange countries
at which she looks in wonder.

5 Post card: Carte Postale

They are alone here,
three of them in black and white.
No-one is smiling.
The children huddle in
on either side, strained and doubtful.
Their hair is longer
but hers has lost its fulness.
It is darker, firmer, moulded to the head.
She wears a heavy overdress
with narrow skirt and frog fastening.
On the edge of the chair
she perches uncomfortably
feet awkwardly cramped.

Still in the sombre face
the deep-set eyes hold their different angles;
one that looks directly at you,
the other gazing through you far away
to some quite different world.

Their mourning figures encode grief.

Whose death are we looking at?

She stares into the nineteen-twenties
holding those nervous daughters to her side.
I feel my mother's tentative arm around me,
her left hand grasping mine.

ANGELA COSTEN

Manifesto on *Ars Poetica*

My poetry is exacting a confession
from me: I will not keep the truth
from my song and the heartstringed instrument;
The voice undressed by the bees,
I will not bar the voice undressed by the bees
from entering the gourd of my bow-harp.
I will not wash the blood off the image
I will let it flow from the gullet
slit by the assassin's dagger through
the run-on line until it rages in the verbs of terror;
And I will distil life into the horrible adjectives;
I will not clean the poem to impress the tyrant
I will not bend my verses into the bow of a praise song.
I will put the symbols of murder hidden in high offices
in the center of my crude lines of accusations.
I will undress our raped land and expose her wounds.
I will pierce the silence around our land with sharp metaphors
And I will point the light of my poems into the dark
nooks where our people are pounded to pulp.
I will not coat my words in lumps of sugar
I will serve them to our people with the bitter quinine:
I will not keep the truth from my heartstringed guitar;
I will thread the voice from the broken lips
through my volatile verbs that burn the lies.
I will ask only that the poem watch the world closely;
I will ask only that the image put a lamp on the dark
ceiling in the dark sky of my land and light the dirt.
Today, my poetry has exacted a confession from me.

FRANK CHIPASULA

Murdered Lovers' Bodies Disappear in the Night

A modern-day
Shakespearean play
Has ended in a mystery;
Love united Serb and Moslem,
Now in death no-one can find them.

Once they lay in No-Man's Land,
Killed while running hand in hand
From Sarajevo
Land of war
The victims of religion's law.

But overnight they each were stolen,
(One to Serb
And one to Moslem?)
So in death they separate,
Killed in love
By those who hate.

JONATHAN LLOYD

Not My Best Side

i   Not my best side, I'm afraid.
    The artist didn't give me a chance to
    Pose properly, and as you can see,
    Poor chap, he had this obsession with
    Triangles, so he left off two of my
    Feet. I didn't comment at the time
    (What, after all, are two feet
    To a monster?) but afterwards
    I was sorry for the bad publicity.
    Why, I said to myself, should my conqueror
    Be so ostentatiously beardless, and ride
    A horse with a deformed neck and square hoofs?
    Why should my victim be so
    Unattractive as to be inedible,
    And why should she have me literally
    On a string? I don't mind dying
    Ritually, since I always rise again,
    But I should have liked a little more blood
    To show they were taking me seriously.

ii It's hard for a girl to be sure if
    She wants to be rescued. I mean, I quite
    Took to the dragon. It's nice to be
    Liked, if you know what I mean. He was
    So nicely physical, with his claws
    And lovely green skin, and that sexy tail,
    And the way he looked at me,
    He made me feel he was all ready to
    Eat me. And any girl enjoys that.
    So when this boy turned up, wearing machinery,
    On a really *dangerous* horse, to be honest,
    I didn't much fancy him. I mean,
    What was he like underneath the hardware?
    He might have acne, blackheads or even
    Bad breath for all I could tell, but the dragon –
    Well, you could see all his equipment
    At a glance. Still, what could I do?
    The dragon got himself beaten by the boy,
    And a girl's got to think of her future.

iii I have diplomas in Dragon
   Management and Virgin Reclamation.
   My horse is the latest model, with
   Automatic transmission and built-in
   Obsolescence. My spear is custom-built,
   And my prototype armour
   Still on the secret list. You can't
   Do better than me at the moment.
   I'm qualified and equipped to the
   Eyebrow. So why be difficult?
   Don't you want to be killed and/or rescued
   In the most contemporary way? Don't
   You want to carry out the roles
   That sociology and myth have designed for you?
   Don't you realise that, by being choosy,
   You are endangering job-prospects
   In the spear- and horse-building industries?
   What, in any case, does it matter what
   You want? You're in my way.

U. A. FANTHORPE

TV

This is your rectangle of narratives.
This is the voice that saves you from silence.

This is your scroll of perpetual images.
Listen, is there time for the poem to grow
in this incessant noise?

Is there time for that which is secret
to blossom?

Privacy must be paid for.

The blessed room, the refuge, the well, must be paid for.

When the comedians fade like ghosts grimacing in water
when the clowns remove their eyes,

the silence must be paid for, like water,
and the cell be precious

with silence, with fragrance, with the stone of privacy.

For the din is dreadful, the confusion of narratives is merciless,
the screen is vicious, it is a stadium of assassinations.

We need the bubbles of our own secret recesses,
the scent of clear water.

The narratives overwhelm us, they have no meaning, they have no
  connection with each other
We need the sacred light of the imagination.

We need the sacred cell and the pen that lies on the table.
We need the paper, that cool rectangle of white.

For one is heaven and sometimes the other is hell,
the world of frustrated murderers, the advertisements, the elegies
  without echo,
the questioners bending down to the bandaged ones,
the smiling humourless clowns.

The narratives overwhelm us, we need the white paper, unclouded,
we need in that furious hubbub a space for our names,
the sanity of prudent distance.

IAIN CRICHTON SMITH

Bone
and Stone

Song of the Battery Hen

We can't grumble about accommodation:
we have a new concrete floor that's
always dry, four walls that are
painted white, and a sheet-iron roof
the rain drums on. A fan blows warm air
beneath our feet to disperse the smell
of chicken-shit and, on dull days,
fluorescent lighting sees us.

You can tell me: if you come by
the North door, I am in the twelfth pen
on the left-hand side of the third row
from the floor; and in that pen
I am usually the middle one of three.
But, even without directions, you'd
discover me. I have the same orange-
red comb, yellow beak and auburn
feathers, but as the door opens and you
hear above the electric fan a kind of
one-word wail, I am the one
who sounds the loudest in my head.

Listen. Outside this house there's an
orchard with small moss-green apple
trees; beyond that, two fields of
cabbages; then, on the far side of
the road, a broiler house. Listen:
one cockerel crows out of there, as
tall and proud as the first hour of sun.
Sometimes I stop calling with the others
to listen, and wonder if he hears me.

The next time you come here, look for me.
Notice the way I sound inside my head.
God made us all quite differently,
and blessed us with this expensive home.

EDWIN BROCK

Neighbours

That spring was late. We watched the sky
and studied charts for shouldering isobars.
Birds were late to pair. Crows drank from the lamb's eye.

Over Finland small birds fell: song-thrushes
steering north, smudged signatures on light,
migrating warblers, nightingales.

Wing-beats failed over fjords, each lung a sip of gall.
Children were warned of their dangerous beauty.
Milk was spilt in Poland. Each quarrel

the blowback from some old story,
a mouthful of bitter air from the Ukraine
brought by the wind out of its box of sorrows.

This spring a lamb sips caesium on a Welsh hill.
A child, lifting her face to drink the rain,
takes into her blood the poisoned arrow.

Now we are all neighbourly, each little town
in Europe twinned to Chernobyl, each heart
with the burnt fireman, the child on the Moscow train.

In the democracy of the virus and the toxin
we wait. We watch for bird migrations,
one bird returning with green in its voice,

glasnost,
golau glas,
a first break of blue.

GILLIAN CLARKE

golau glas: blue light (Welsh)

The Crayfish

I paid the fisherman on the sands,
And took the horrible brute in my hands,
A dubious being, a thing of the marge,
Hydra in small, wood-louse in large,
Formless as midnight, nameless as God.
It opened a gullet ugly and odd,
And tried to bite me; there came out
From its carapace a sort of snout;
God in the fearful order of Nature
Gave a dim place to the hideous creature;
It tried to bite me; we struggled hard;
It snapped my fingers – on their guard!
But the seller was scarcely out of sight
Behind a cliff, when it got its bite.
So I said, 'Live on and be blessed, poor beast,'
And cast it into the seething yeast,
Setting it free to depart and tell
To the murmuring ocean where it fell
The christening font of the rising sun,
That good, for ill, had once been done
By a human crab to a scaly one!

VICTOR HUGO

Translated by Sir George Young

The Hill Pines ...

The hill pines were sighing,
O'ercast and chill was the day:
A mist in the valley lying
Blotted the pleasant May.

But deep in the glen's bosom
Summer slept in the fire
Of the odorous gorse-blossom
And the hot scent of the brier.

A ribald cuckoo clamoured,
And out of the corpse the stroke
Of the iron axe that hammered
The iron heart of the oak.

Anon a sound appalling,
As a hundred years of pride
Crashed, in the silence falling:
And the shadowy pine-trees sighed.

ROBERT BRIDGES

From: *The Brook*

I wind about, and in and out,
  With here a blossom sailing,
And here and there a lusty trout,
  And here and there a grayling.

And here and there a foamy flake
  Upon me, as I travel
With many a silvery waterbreak
  Above the golden gravel,

And draw them all along, and flow
  To join the brimming river,
For men may come and men may go,
  But I go on for ever.

LORD TENNYSON

The Magpie's Son

Those wary pirates of the apple-trees
and hayfield, making awkward strut,
this year have with them their pied fledgling,
black sword-beak prodding and already sleek
in white and jet and sapphire, tufted scut
– the vestige of his youth – not yet a blade
to saw the wind, as their rasp-voices
shred summer's silence.

When they are feeding – these bird tyrants –
others fly, a twitter of concern
for blue-pearl eggs and tender fluff-bloom young.
I hated then, like finch or wren or sparrow
crouching in the thorn, until I found him
– an end before beginning of his thieving –
laid in the lane, a trickle of cooled blood,
and held him in my hand – the magpie's son –

and I was grieving.

SHEILA GLEN BISHOP

Pied Beauty

Glory be to God for dappled things –
    For skies of couple-colour as a brinded cow;
        For rose-moles all in stipple upon trout that swim;
Fresh-firecoal chestnut-falls; finches' wings;
    Landscape plotted and pieced – fold, fallow, and plough;
        And áll trádes, their gear and tackle and trim.

All things counter, original, spare, strange;
    Whatever is fickle, freckled (who knows how?)
        With swift, slow; sweet, sour; adazzle, dim;
He fathers-forth whose beauty is past change:
            Praise him.

GERARD MANLEY HOPKINS

Digging

Today I think
Only with scents, – scents dead leaves yield,
And bracken, and wild carrot's seed,
And the square mustard field;

Odours that rise
When the spade wounds the root of tree,
Rose, currant, raspberry, or goutweed,
Rhubarb or celery;

The smoke's smell, too
Flowing from where a bonfire burns
The dead, the waste, the dangerous,
And all to sweetness turns.

It is enough
To smell, to crumble the dark earth,
While the robin sings over again
Sad songs of Autumn mirth.

EDWARD THOMAS

Special Green

They suit a life completely
unlike this, the owls, seals,
porcupines. The emu strides from stake

to stake. Queuing parrots bicker.
Wildcats tremble in their sleep.
An alligator opens its mouth,

not feeling the wind, not fearing
the yelling aeroplanes that slope
to the distance like blips.

An arctic fox shakes sand away,
yawns: a raccoon lifts pips
from a knife-quartered pear,

gentle, accurate as tweezers.
It eats, eyelids lowered inside
its mask, then climbs a ladder

into a barrel. The wood is stained
fern-green, in preservative specially
mixed to do raccoons no harm.

ROBERT ETTY

The White Tiger

It was beautiful as God
must be beautiful; glacial
eyes that had looked on
violence and come to terms

with it; a body too huge
and majestic for the cage in which
it had been put; up
and down in the shadow

of its own bulk it went,
lifting, as it turned,
the crumpled flower of its face
to look into my own

face without seeing me. It
was the colour of the moonlight
on snow and as quiet
as moonlight, but breathing

as you can imagine that
God breathes within the confines
of our definition of him, agonising
over immensities that will not return.

R. S. THOMAS

The Trees Are Down

> – and he cried with a loud voice:
> Hurt not the earth, neither the sea, nor the trees – (Revelation)

They are cutting down the great plane-trees at the end of the garden.
    For days there has been the grate of the saw, the swish of the
        branches as they fall,
The crash of trunks, the rustle of trodden leaves,
With the 'Whoops' and the 'Whoas', the loud common talk, the
    loud common laughs of the men, above it all.

I remember one evening of a long past Spring
Turning in at a gate, getting out of a cart, and finding a large
    dead rat in the mud of the drive.
I remember thinking: alive or dead, a rat was a god-forsaken thing,
But at least, in May, that even a rat should be alive.
The week's work here is as good as done. There is just one bough
    On the roped bole, in the fine grey rain,
        Green and high
        And lonely against the sky.
            (Down now!–)
        And but for that,
        If an old dead rat
Did once, for a moment, unmake the Spring, I might never have
    thought of him again.

It is not for a moment the Spring is unmade to-day;
These were great trees, it was in them from root to stem:
When the men with the 'Whoops' and the 'Whoas' have carted
    the whole of the whispering loveliness away
Half the Spring, for me, will have gone with them.

It is going now, and my heart has been struck with the hearts of
   the planes;
Half my life it has beat with these, in the sun, in the rains,
      In the March wind, the May breeze,
In the great gales that came over to them across the roofs from
   the great seas.
        There was only a quiet rain when they were dying;
        They must have heard the sparrows flying,
And the small creeping creatures in the earth where they were lying –
        But I, all day, I heard an angel crying:
          'Hurt not the trees'.

CHARLOTTE MEW

Distance Collapsed in Rubble

Distance collapsed in rubble and time was shaken,
the devil of speed stamped on the brows
of great mountains and reversed the river's flow,
the seed lay poisoned in the earth,
the sap flowed poisoned in the stem.
A mighty generation of people died out
but everyone knew that the time was very near.

ANNA AKHMATOVA

Translated by Richard McKane

Permafrost

For all frozen things –
my middle finger that whitens
from its old, ten-minute frostbite,

for black, slimy potatoes
left in the clamp,
for darkness and cold like cloths
over the cage,

for permafrost, lichen crusts
nuzzled by reindeer,
the tender balance of decades
null as a vault.

For all frozen things –
the princess and princes
staring out of their bunker
at the original wind,

for NATO survivors in nuclear moonsuits
whirled from continent to continent

like Okies in bumpy Fords
fleeing the dustbowl.

For all frozen things –
snowdrops and Christmas roses
blasted down to the germ
of their genetic zip-code.

They fly by memory –
cargo of endless winter,
clods of celeriac, chipped
turnips, lanterns at ten a.m.

in the gloom of a Finnish market-place;
flowers under glass, herring,
little wizened apples.

For all frozen things –
the nipped fish in a mess of ice,
the uncovered galleon
tossed from four centuries of memory,

for nuclear snowsuits bouncing on dust,
trapped on the rough ride of the earth's surface,
on the rough swing of its axis,

like moon-men lost on the moon
watching the earth's green flush

tremble and perish.

HELEN DUNMORE

Augury

The fish faced into the current,
Its mouth agape,
Its whole head opened like a valve.
You said 'It's diseased.'

A pale crusted sore
Turned like a coin
And wound to the bottom,
Unsettling silt off a weed.

We hang charmed
On the trembling catwalk:
What can fend us now
Can soothe the hurt eye

Of the sun,
Unpoison great lakes,
Turn back
The rat on the road.

SEAMUS HEANEY

Binsey Poplars

felled 1879

My aspens dear, whose airy cages quelled,
Quelled or quenched in leaves the leaping sun,
All felled, felled, are all felled;
   Of a fresh and following folded rank
        Not spared, not one
        That dandled a sandalled
     Shadow that swam or sank
On meadow and river and wind-wandering weed-winding bank.

O if we knew what we do
      When we delve or hew –
   Hack and rack the growing green!
     Since country is so tender
To touch, her being só slender,
That, like this sleek and seeing ball
But a prick will make no eye at all,
Where we, even where we mean
       To mend her we end her,
   When we hew or delve:
After-comers cannot guess the beauty been.
  Ten or twelve, only ten or twelve
    Strokes of havoc únselve
     The sweet especial scene,
   Rural scene, a rural scene,
   Sweet especial rural scene.

GERARD MANLEY HOPKINS

Pigeons

Pigeons perch on the Holy Family
Carved over the west door on Joseph's head

On Mary's hand, making them smirk like humans
Who are kind to animals. Inside

The church now, we look out: the birds
Fly through the brown and scarlet saints, and crawl

Like sleepy wasps against their sandalled feet,
Lords of the window, devils looking in.

Then from the street a backfire sends them packing,
Only the stolid and the deaf stay on –

The saints are left to bow. The pigeons' wings
Clap round the square like faraway applause.

PATRICIA BEER

Snow

The room was suddenly rich and the great bay-window was
Spawning snow and pink roses against it
Soundlessly collateral and incompatible:
World is suddener than we fancy it.

World is crazier and more of it than we think,
Incorrigibly plural. I peel and portion
A tangerine and spit the pips and feel
The drunkenness of things being various.

And the fire flames with a bubbling sound for world
Is more spiteful and gay than one supposes –
On the tongue on the eyes on the ears in the palms of one's hands –
There is more than glass between the snow and the huge roses.

LOUIS MacNEICE

Mountain Lion

Climbing through the January snow, into the Lobo canyon
Dark grow the spruce-trees, blue is the balsam, water sounds
    still unfrozen, and the trail is still evident.

Men!
Two men!
Men! The only animal in the world to fear!

They hesitate.
We hesitate.
They have a gun.
We have no gun.

Then we all advance, to meet.

Two Mexicans, strangers, emerging out of the dark and snow
    and inwardness of the Lobo valley.
What are they doing here on this vanishing trail?

What is he carrying?
Something yellow.
A deer?

Qué tiene, amigo?
Léon –

He smiles, foolishly, as if he were caught doing wrong.
And we smile, foolishly, as if we didn't know.
He is quite gentle and dark-faced.

It is a mountain lion.
A long, long slim cat, yellow like a lioness.
Dead.

He trapped her this morning, he says, smiling foolishly.

Lift up her face,
Her round, bright face, bright as frost.
Her round, fine-fashioned head, with two dead ears;
And stripes in the brilliant frost of her face, sharp, fine dark rays,
Dark, keen, fine rays in the brilliant frost of her face.
Beautiful dead eyes.

Hermoso es!

They go out towards the open;
We go on into the gloom of Lobo.
And above the trees I found her lair,
A hole in the blood-orange brilliant rocks that stick up, a little cave.

And bones, and twigs, and a perilous ascent.
So, she will never leap up that way again, with the yellow flash
   of a mountain lion's long shoot!
And her bright striped frost-face will never watch any more, out
   of the shadow of the cave in the blood-orange rock,
Above the trees of the Lobo dark valley-mouth!

Instead, I look out.
And out to the dim of the desert, like a dream, never real;
To the snow of the Sangre de Cristo mountains, the ice
   of the mountains of Picoris,
And near across at the opposite steep of snow, green trees
   motionless standing in snow, like a Christmas toy.

And I think in this empty world there was room for me
   and a mountain lion.
And I think in the world beyond, how easily we might spare a
   million or two of humans
And never miss them.
Yet what a gap in the world, the missing white frost-face of that
   slim yellow mountain lion!

D. H. LAWRENCE

Qué tiene, amigo?	What have you got friend?
Léon –	A lion –
Hermoso es!	It is beautiful!

The Cock

from: *The Nun's Priest's Tale*

A yeerd she hadde, enclosed al aboute
With stikkes, and a drye dych withoute,
In which she hadde a cok, hight Chauntecleer.
In al the land, of crowyng nas his peer.
His voys was murier than the murie orgon
On messe-dayes that in the chirche gon.
Wel sikerer was his crowying in his logge
Than is a clokke or an abbey orlogge.
By nature he knew ech ascencioun
Of the equynoxial in thilke toun;
For whan degrees fiftene weren ascended,
Thanne crew he, that it myghte nat been amended.
His coomb was redder than the fyn coral,
And batailled as it were a castel wal;
His byle was blak, and as the jeet it shoon;
Lyk asure were his legges and his toon;
His nayles whitter than the lylye flour,
And lyk the burned gold was his colour.
This gentil cok hadde in his governaunce
Sevene hennes for to doon al his plesaunce,
Whiche were his sustres and his paramours,
And wonder lyk to hym, as of colours;
Of whiche the fairest hewed on hir throte
Was cleped faire damoysel Pertelote.

GEOFFREY CHAUCER

Fallow Deer at the Lonely House

One without looks in to-night
    Through the curtain-chink
From the sheet of glistening white;
One without looks in to-night
    As we sit and think
    By the fender-brink.

We do not discern those eyes
    Watching in the snow;
Lit by lamps of rosy dyes
We do not discern those eyes
    Wondering, aglow,
    Fourfooted, tiptoe.

THOMAS HARDY

Mice Before Milk

from: *The Manciple's Tale*

Lat take a cat and fostre hym wel with milk
And tendre flessch and make his couch of silk,
And lat hym seen a mouse go by the wal,
Anon he weyvith milk and flessch and all,
And every deyntee that is in that hous,
Suich appetit he hath to ete a mous.

GEOFFREY CHAUCER

The Fly

Little Fly,
Thy summer's play
My thoughtless hand
Has brush'd away.

Am not I
A fly like thee?
Or art not thou
A man like me?

For I dance,
And drink, and sing,
Till some blind hand
Shall brush my wing.

WILLIAM BLAKE

On Finding a Small Fly Crushed in a Book

Some hand, that never meant to do thee hurt,
Has crush'd thee here between these pages pent;
But thou has left thine own fair monument,
Thy wings gleam out and tell me what thou wert:
Oh! that the memories, which survive us here,
Were half as lovely as these wings of thine!
Pure relics of a blameless life, that shine
Now thou art gone: Our doom is ever near:
The peril is beside us day by day;
The book will close upon us, it may be,
Just as we lift ourselves to soar away
Upon the summer-airs. But, unlike thee,
The closing book may stop our vital breath,
Yet leave no lustre on our page of death.

CHARLES TENNYSON TURNER

The Shark

A treacherous monster is the Shark,
He never makes the least remark.

And when he sees you on the sand,
He doesn't seem to want to land.

He watches you take off your clothes,
And not the least excitement shows.

His eyes do not grow bright or roll,
He has astounding self-control.

He waits till you are quite undrest,
And seems to take no interest.

And when towards the sea you leap,
He looks as if he were asleep.

But when you once get in his range,
His whole demeanour seems to change.

He throws his body right about,
And his true character comes out.

It's no use crying or appealing,
He seems to lose all decent feeling.

After this warning you will wish
To keep clear of this treacherous fish.

His back is black, his stomach white,
He has a very dangerous bite.

LORD ALFRED DOUGLAS

A Holiday

My child in the smoke of the fire
playing at barbarism,
the burst meat dripping down her
chin, soot smearing
her cheek and her hair infested with twigs,
under a huge midsummer-leafed tree
in the rain, the shelter
of poles and canvas down
the road if needed:

This could be where we
end up, learning the minimal
with maybe no tree, no rain,
no shelter, no roast carcasses
of animals to renew us

at a time when language
will shrink to the word *hunger*
and the word *none*.

Mist lifts from the warm lake
hit by the cold drizzle:
too much dust in the stratosphere
this year, they say. Unseasonal.

Here comes the ice,
here comes something,
we can all feel it
like a breath, a footstep,
here comes nothing
with its calm eye of fire.

What we're having right
now is a cookout,
sausages on peeled sticks.
The blades of grass are still with us.
My daughter forages,
grace plumps the dusty berries,
two or three hot and squashed in her fist.

So far we do it
for fun. So far is
where we've gone
and no farther.

MARGARET ATWOOD

Runaway

It was dark when we came home,
door still jammed as if she'd shut it
behind her, covered her tracks.
A cold black doglessness.

It's hard to say what I missed most:
waggish ears; her casual furstyle;
polished eyes under politician's brows;
her Guinness jig; tabor of her tail;
or that bark I could pick out
a bone's throw from Battersea Dogs' Home.

But nothing. Nothing but a flat tangle
of straw, a half-eaten dish of Poacher's.
We spent all evening not talking about dogs,
seeming to listen to the jazz on Radio 3,
tuned in to the wind growling at the curtains.

Midnight kept us awake
till a small canine voice called
to us to open the door, like a teenage son
who'd forgotten his key. She was pure skulk
until she remembered she was our best friend.
And that was what her tongue was for.

LINDA FRANCE

Kankaria Lake

Sometimes the nine-year-old boy
finds it difficult
to believe this is water.

It is more like skin;
a reptile's skin –
wrinkled and rough as a crocodile's and green.

Bacterial green, decomposed
green – opaque and dull.

As if the lake
were a giant crocodile
he couldn't see the ends of.

Kankaria Lake is on the way
to the Ahmedabad Zoo.
Sundays he always walks across
the bridge over the lake.

In the distance he can see
a small park bordered
          by the water – dry grass
struggles to grow against the scummy lake.
The park seems always deserted.

Sometimes a gardener
or a homeless man
or a wandering storyteller
would fall asleep on the grass
                    too close to the lake –
and soon enough the newspapers
would report about how
the crocodiles had devoured
yet another careless man.

The boy thinks he would like to witness
                    such an event.

But then, would he try
          to save the man?

He's not sure.

Or would he just watch
to see how a crocodile eats?

Would the man's legs go first
        or the arms
        or the stomach?

The boy imagines the lake
overpopulated with crocodiles
who never have enough to eat –
for he doesn't believe any fish
could live in such water.

There are hardly any trees
near the lake; no friendly monkeys
who would throw fruits down
to the crocodiles, as they do
        in one old story …

Kankaria Lake had also become
the most popular place
for suicides – That was a fact
which felt more like science-fiction
        to him.

On those Sunday afternoon
                family outings
he stops
in the middle of the bridge
and leans out
    towards the lake,
now and then sticking his legs out
through the railing
hoping at least one crocodile
will surface,
    raise its head.

But no.
Nothing ever happens.
Sometimes the wind pokes
the lake, making murky ripples.
But the crocodiles prefer
to remain hidden below.
How do they breathe?
      He worries.

In the end he was
always marched off
disappointed to the zoo
where he faced sullen animals
sometimes crouched far away
in the darkest part of the cage,
frightened in
   their festering skins.

SUJATA BHATT

One Another

I'm Really Very Fond

I'm really very fond of you,
he said.

I don't like fond.
It sounds like something
you would tell a dog.

Give me love,
or nothing.

Throw your fond in a pond,
I said.

But what I felt for him
was also warm, frisky,
moist-mouthed,
eager,
and could swim away

if forced to do so.

ALICE WALKER

Walker

When I no longer have your heart
I will not request your body
your presence
or even your polite conversation.
I will go away to a far country
separated from you by the sea
– on which I cannot walk –
and refrain even from sending
letters
describing my pain.

ALICE WALKER

First Love

I ne'er was struck before that hour
    With love so sudden and so sweet.
Her face it bloomed like a sweet flower
    And stole my heart away complete.
My face turned pale as deadly pale,
    My legs refused to walk away,
And when she looked 'what could I ail?'
    My life and all seemed turned to clay.

And then my blood rushed to my face
    And took my sight away.
The trees and bushes round the place
    Seemed midnight at noonday.
I could not see a single thing,
    Words from my eyes did start;
They spoke as chords do from the string
    And blood burnt round my heart.

Are flowers the winter's choice?
    Is love's bed always snow?
She seemed to hear my silent voice
    And love's appeal to know.
I never saw so sweet a face
    As that I stood before:
My heart has left its dwelling-place
    And can return no more.

JOHN CLARE

To Marguerite

Yes! in the sea of life enisled,
With echoing straits between us thrown,
Dotting the shoreless watery wild,
We mortal millions live *alone*.
The islands feel the enclasping flow,
And then their endless bounds they know.

But when the moon their hollows lights,
And they are swept by balms of spring,
And in their glens, on starry nights,
The nightingales divinely sing;
And lovely notes, from shore to shore,
Across the sounds and channels pour –

Oh! then a longing like despair
Is to their farthest caverns sent;
For surely once, they feel, we were
Parts of a single continent!
Now round us spreads the watery plain –
Oh might our marges meet again!

Who order'd, that their longing's fire
Should be, as soon as kindled, cool'd?
Who renders vain their deep desire? –
A God, a God their severance ruled;
And bade betwixt their shores to be
The unplumb'd, salt, estranging sea.

MATTHEW ARNOLD

A Kiss

O, that joy so soon should waste!
　Or so sweet a bliss
　　As a kiss,
Might not forever last!
So sugared, so melting, so soft, so delicious,
　The dew that lies on roses,
　　When the morn herself discloses,
　　　Is not so precious.
O, rather than I would it smother,
Were I to taste such another;
　It should be my wishing
　That I might die kissing.

BEN JONSON

One Flesh

Lying apart now, each in a separate bed,
He with a book, keeping the light on late,
She like a girl dreaming of childhood,
All men elsewhere – it is as if they wait
Some new event: the book he holds unread,
Her eyes fixed on the shadows overhead.

Tossed up like flotsam from a former passion,
How cool they lie. They hardly ever touch,
Or if they do it is like a confession
Of having little feeling – or too much.
Chastity faces them, a destination
For which their whole lives were a preparation.

Strangely apart, yet strangely close together,
Silence between them like a thread to hold
And not wind in. And time itself's a feather
Touching them gently. Do they know they're old,
These two who are my father and my mother
Whose fire from which I came, has now grown cold?

ELIZABETH JENNINGS

Anniversaries

The Fourth

Anniversary weather: I drive
under a raw sunset, the road
cramped between drifts, hedges
polished into sharp crests.

I have it by heart now;
on this day in each year
no signposts point anywhere
but east into Essex,

and so to your ward,
where snow recovers tonight
the ground I first saw lost
four winters ago.

Whatever time might bring,
all my journeys take me
back to this dazzling dark:
I watch my shadow ahead

plane across open fields,
out of my reach for ever,
but setting towards your bed
to find itself waiting there.

ANDREW MOTION

Sonnet

I wish I could remember that first day,
First hour, first moment of your meeting me,
If bright or dim the season, it might be
Summer or Winter for aught I can say;
So unrecorded did it slip away,
So blind was I to see and to foresee,
So dull to mark the budding of my tree
That would not blossom yet for many a May.
If only I could recollect it, such
A day of days! I let it come and go
As traceless as a thaw of bygone snow;
It seemed to mean so little, meant so much;
If only now I could recall that touch,
First touch of hand in hand – Did one but know!

CHRISTINA ROSSETTI

Shall I Compare Thee ...?

Shall I compare thee to a summer's day?
Thou art more lovely and more temperate:
Rough winds do shake the darling buds of May,
And summer's lease hath all too short a date:
Sometime too hot the eye of heaven shines,
And often is his gold complexion dimm'd;
And every fair from fair sometime declines,
By chance, or Nature's changing course, untrimm'd;
But thy eternal summer shall not fade,
Nor lose possession of that fair thou owest;
Nor shall Death brag thou wander'st in his shade,
When in eternal lines to time thou growest;
    So long as men can breathe, or eyes can see,
    So long lives this, and this gives life to thee.

WILLIAM SHAKESPEARE

People Etcetera

People are lovely to touch –
A nice warm sloppy tilting belly
Happy in its hollow of pelvis
Like a bowl of porridge.

People are fun to notice –
Their eyes taking off like birds
Away from their words
To settle on breasts and ankles
Irreverent as pigeons.

People are good to smell –
Leathery, heathery, culinary or Chanel,
Lamb's-wool, sea-salt, linen dried in the wind,
Skin fresh out of a shower.

People are delicious to taste –
Crisp and soft and tepid as new-made bread,
Tangy as blackberries, luscious as avocado,
Native as milk,
Acrid as truth.

People are irresistible to draw –
Hand following hand,
Eye outstaring eye,
Every curve an experience of self,
Felt weight of flesh, tension of muscle
And all the geology of an elderly face.

And people are easy to write about?
Don't say it.
What are these shadows
Vanishing
Round the
Corner?

ELMA MITCHELL

A Blade of Grass

You ask for a poem.
I offer you a blade of grass.
You say it is not good enough.
You ask for a poem.

I say this blade of grass will do.
It has dressed itself in frost,
It is more immediate
Than any image of my making.

You say it is not a poem.
It is a blade of grass and grass
Is not quite good enough.
I offer you a blade of grass.

You are indignant.
You say it is too easy to offer grass.
It is absurd.
Anyone can offer a blade of grass.

You ask for a poem.
And so I write you a tragedy about
How a blade of grass
Becomes more and more difficult to offer,

And about how as you grow older
A blade of grass
Becomes more difficult to accept.

BRIAN PATTEN

In Our Tenth Year

This book, this page, this harebell laid to rest
between these sheets, these leaves, if pressed still bleeds
a watercolour of the way we were.

Those years: the fuss of such and such a day,
that disagreement and its final word,
your inventory of names and dates and times,
my infantries of tall, dark, handsome lies.

A decade on, now we astound ourselves;
still two, still twinned but doubled now with love
and for a single night apart, alone,
how sure we are, each of the other half.

This harebell holds its own. Let's give it now
in air, in light, the chance to fade, to fold.
Here, take it from my hand. Now, let it go.

SIMON ARMITAGE

The Rose

Such concentration on a single rose,
you look as though you watch it breathe the scent
till I am watching you and held intent,
your breath so hushed it hardly comes or goes.
What does it say to hold you in that pose,
that my lips cannot move, my hands invent?
Your words, they never tell me what is meant;
my hands can't touch the peace your body knows.

Pale bloom that gathers light from dusk, your hand
as white as whittled hazel without shine,
the sill and window where you hold quite still.
A word could break the spell. I ache to stand
in for your eyes and grasp this rose in mine
as closely as your hand along the sill.

PETER DALE

The Hill

Breathless, we flung us on the windy hill,
   Laughed in the sun, and kissed the lovely grass.
   You said, 'Through glory and ecstasy we pass;
Wind, sun, and earth remain, the birds sing still,
When we are old, are old…' 'And when we die
   All's over that is ours; and life burns on
Through other lovers, other lips,' said I,
   'Heart of my heart, our heaven is now, is won!'

'We are Earth's best, that learnt her lesson here.
   Life is our cry. We kept the faith!' we said;
   'We shall go down with unreluctant tread
Rose-crowned into the darkness!'… Proud we were,
   And laughed, that had such brave true things to say
   – And then you suddenly cried, and turned away.

RUPERT BROOKE

Flying Saucer

She sent it by hand
from the heart
to the head.
It ended by my feet
in sorry smithereens.
Overarm discus champ
I never knew
the grace, the power,
what aim!
Encourage talent say I,
so stood and goaded
while she launched
The Ceramic Age.
Enough
turn and run,
not fast enough –
'Flying Saucer Completes Successful Moon Shot'.

JOHN HAWKHEAD

Sonnet

Time does not bring relief; you all have lied
Who told me time would ease me of my pain!
I miss him in the weeping of the rain;
I want him at the shrinking of the tide;
The old snows melt from every mountain-side,
And last year's leaves are smoke in every lane;
But last year's bitter loving must remain
Heaped on my heart, and my old thoughts abide.
There are a hundred places where I fear
To go, – so with his memory they brim.
And entering with relief some quiet place
Where never fell his foot or shone his face
I say, 'There is no memory of him here!'
And so stand stricken, so remembering him.

EDNA ST VINCENT MILLAY

The Marriage of True Minds

Let me not to the marriage of true minds
Admit impediments. Love is not love
Which alters when it alteration finds,
Or bends with the remover to remove:
O, no! it is an ever-fixèd mark,
That looks on tempests and is never shaken;
It is the star to every wandering bark,
Whose worth's unknown, although his height be taken.
Love's not Time's fool, though rosy lips and cheeks
Within his bending sickle's compass come;
Love alters not with his brief hours and weeks,
But bears it out even to the edge of doom.
If this be error, and upon me prov'd,
I never writ, nor no man ever lov'd.

WILLIAM SHAKESPEARE

You Were Saying?

'I love you'

Can you repeat that,
a thought just caught me,
not much of a thought,
just enough to lose your words
in a confusion of background music
filtered through a shopping arcade.

'I love you'

Pardon, God these people!

1lb of sugar	butter
greens	bread
potatoes	pepper
cooking oil	chicken

You were saying

'Nothing, it's not important'

Suit yourself.

PATRICIA AND JOHN HAWKHEAD

From: *To His Coy Mistress*

Had we but world enough, and time,
This coyness, Lady, were no crime.
We would sit down, and think which way
To walk, and pass our long love's day.
Thou by the Indian Ganges' side
Shouldst rubies find: I by the tide
Of Humber would complain. I would
Love you ten years before the flood:
And you should, if you please, refuse
Till the conversion of the Jews.
My vegetable love should grow
Vaster than empires, and more slow.
An hundred years should go to praise
Thine eyes, and on thy forehead gaze.
Two hundred to adore each breast:
But thirty thousand to the rest.
An age at least to every part,
And the last age should show your heart;
For, Lady, you deserve this state;
Nor would I love at lower rate.
   But at my back I always hear
Time's wingèd chariot hurrying near:
And yonder all before us lie
Deserts of vast eternity.
Thy beauty shall no more be found;
Nor, in thy marble vault, shall sound
My echoing song: then worms shall try
That long-preserved virginity:
And your quaint honour turn to dust
And into ashes all my lust.
The grave's a fine and private place,
But none, I think, do there embrace.

ANDREW MARVELL

Follower

My father worked with a horse-plough,
His shoulders globed like a full sail strung
Between the shafts and the furrow.
The horses strained at his clicking tongue.

An expert. He would set the wing
And fit the bright steel-pointed sock.
The sod rolled over without breaking.
At the headrig, with a single pluck

Of reins, the sweating team turned round
And back into the land. His eye
Narrowed and angled at the ground,
Mapping the furrow exactly.

I stumbled in his hob-nailed wake,
Fell sometimes on the polished sod;
Sometimes he rode me on his back
Dipping and rising to his plod.

I wanted to grow up and plough,
To close one eye, stiffen my arm.
All I ever did was follow
In his broad shadow round the farm.

I was a nuisance, tripping, falling,
Yapping always. But today
It is my father who keeps stumbling
Behind me, and will not go away.

SEAMUS HEANEY

Brothers

How lovely the elder brother's
Life all laced in the other's,
Lóve-laced! – what once I well
Witnessed; so fortune fell.
When Shrovetide, two years gone,
Our boys' plays brought on
Part was picked for John,
Young Jóhn; then fear, then joy
Ran revel in the elder boy.
Now the night come; all
Our company thronged the hall;
Henry, by the wall,
Beckoned me beside him:
I came where called, and eyed him
By meanwhiles; making mý play
Turn most on tender byplay.
For, wrung all on love's rack,
My lad, and lost in Jack,
Smiled, blushed, and bit his lip;
Or drove, with a diver's dip,
Clutched hands through claspèd knees;
And many a mark like these,
Told tales with what heart's stress
He hung on the imp's success.
Now the other was bráss-bóld:
Hé had no work to hold
His heart up at the strain;
Nay, roguish ran the vein.
Two tedious acts were past;
Jack's call and cue at last;
When Henry, heart-forsook,
Dropped eyes and dared not look.
Thére! the háll rúng!
Dog, he did give tongue!
But Harry – in his hands he has flung
His tear-tricked cheeks of flame
For fond love and for shame.
    Ah Nature, framed in fault,

There's comfort then, there's salt;
Nature, bad, base, and blind,
Dearly thou canst be kind;
There dearly thén, deárly,
Dearly thou canst be kind.

GERARD MANLEY HOPKINS

Registers

Out of the warm primordial cave
of our conversations, Jack's gone.
No more chit-chat under the blankets
pegged over chairs and nipped in drawers.

Throughout his first five years an ear
always open, at worst ajar,
I catch myself still listening out
for sounds of him in the sensible house

where nothing stirs but the washing machine
which clicks and churns. I'm loosening his arms
clasped round my neck, detaching myself
from his soft protracted kiss goodbye.

Good boy, diminishing down the long
corridors into the huge unknown
assembly hall, each word strange,
even his name on Miss Cracknell's tongue.

MICHAEL LASKEY

The Gift

After the accident, the hospital,
they brought me aching home
mouth pumped up like a tyre
black stitches tracking the wound
over my lip, the red slit signalling
the broken place. And my son
my tall, cool son of sixteen
kissed the top of my head
and over the curve of my shoulder
laid his arm, like the broad wing
of a mother bird guarding its young.

Anyone who has known tenderness
thrown like a lifeline into the heart of pain
anyone who has known pain bleed into tenderness
knows how the power of the two combine.
And if I am a fool to give thanks
for pain as well as tenderness
and even if, as some would say
there are no accidents –

Still. I am grateful for the gift.

CHRIS BANKS

Laundrette

We sit nebulous in steam.
It calms the air and makes the windows stream
rippling the hinterland's big houses to a blur
of bedsits – not a patch on what they were before.

We stuff the tub, jam money in the slot,
sit back on rickle chairs not
reading. The paperbacks in our pockets curl.
Our eyes are riveted. Our own colours whirl.

We pour in smithereens of soap. The machine sobs
through its cycle. The rhythm throbs
and changes. Suds drool and slobber in the churn.
Our duds don't know which way to turn.

The dark shoves one man in,
lugging a bundle like a wandering Jew. Linen
washed in public here.
We let out of the bag who we are.

This youngwife has a fine stack of sheets, each pair
a present. She admires their clean cut air
of colourschemes and being chosen. Are the dyes fast?
This christening lather will be the first test.

This woman is deadpan before the rinse and sluice
of the family in a bagwash. Let them stew in their juice
to a final fankle, twisted, wrung out into rope,
hard to unravel. She sees a kaleidoscope

For her to narrow her eyes and blow smoke at, his overalls
and pants ballooning, tangling with her smalls
and the teeshirts skinned from her wriggling son.
She has a weather eye for what might shrink or run.

This dour man does for himself. Before him,
half lost, his small possessions swim.
Cast off, random
they nose and nudge the porthole glass like flotsam.

LIZ LOCHHEAD

Poem for My Sister

My little sister likes to try my shoes,
to strut in them,
admire her spindle-thin twelve-year-old legs
in this season's styles.
She says they fit her perfectly,
but wobbles
on their high heels, they're
hard to balance.

I like to watch my little sister
playing hopscotch, admire the neat hops-and-skips of her,
their quick peck,
never-missing their mark, not
over-stepping the line.
She is competent at peever.

I try to warn my little sister
about unsuitable shoes,
point out my own distorted feet, the callouses,
odd patches of hard skin.
I should not like to see her
in my shoes.
I wish she could stay
sure footed,
      sensibly shod.

LIZ LOCHHEAD

Football after School

(to Kerry)

You'll be one of them in a few years,
warpaint slicked over your face –
your common language jeers,
dribbling the sun about the place
with the premature swagger
of manhood, butting it with your head:
your school tie a stiff striped dagger.

Yes, soon you'll be picking scabs
of kisses off your skin as each kick
makes you dwarf a tree, and stab
a flower; the unset homework
between margins of this makeshift pitch
teaching you more than a textbook
how to survive any monster's switch.

Yet as I look at your porcelain skin,
their granite jowls, I wonder if you'll ever
know how to dodge bruises on your shins
from studded boots, be clever
enough to tackle fouls with something
more than inkstained fists and feet. Perhaps
you'll be too vulnerable for living –

not hooligan enough to trample
into the sod your shadow that grows
twice as fast as yourself, to sample
punches below the belt from one you know
without flinching. I can't prevent
crossbones on your knees
turn bullies into cement –

or confiscate the sun
they'll puncture and put out.
In their robust world I'm no Amazon.
I can only scream inside without a shout
for you not to inherit my fragility:
never to love too much or be aged
as I was by youth's anxiety.

PATRICIA McCARTHY

More Poems

XXXVII

I did not lose my heart in summer's even,
    When roses to the moonrise burst apart:
When plumes were under heel and lead was flying,
    In blood and smoke and flame I lost my heart.

I lost it to a soldier and a foeman,
    A chap that did not kill me, but he tried;
That took the sabre straight and took it striking,
    And laughed and kissed his hand to me and died.

A. E. HOUSMAN

life _and_ Death

Fear No More the Heat of the Sun

From Cymbeline IV ii

Fear no more the heat o' the sun,
    Nor the furious winter's rages;
Thou thy worldly task hast done,
    Home art gone, and ta'en thy wages:
Golden lads and girls all must,
As chimney sweepers, come to dust.

Fear no more the frown o' the great,
    Thou art past the tyrant's stroke;
Care no more to clothe and eat;
    To thee the reed is as the oak:
The sceptre, learning, physic, must
All follow this, and come to dust.

Fear no more the lightning-flash,
    Nor the all-dreaded thunder-stone;
Fear not slander, censure rash;
    Thou hast finished joy and moan:
All lovers young, all lovers must
Consign to thee, and come to dust.

WILLIAM SHAKESPEARE

Lament

We who are left, how shall we look again
Happily on the sun, or feel the rain,
Without remembering how they who went
Ungrudgingly, and spent
Their all for us, loved, too, the sun and rain?

A bird among the rain-wet lilac sings –
But we, how shall we turn to little things
And listen to the birds and winds and streams
Made holy by their dreams,
Nor feel the heart-break in the heart of things?

WILFRED GIBSON

For a Dead African

We have no heroes and no wars
only victims of a sickly state
succumbing to the variegated sores
that flower under lashing rains of hate.

We have no battles and no fights
for history to record with trite remark
only captives killed on eyeless nights
and accidental dyings in the dark.

Yet when the roll of those who died
to free our land is called, without surprise
these nameless unnamed ones will stand beside
the warriors who secured the final prize.

JOHN NANGOZA JEBE

Suicide in the Trenches

I knew a simple soldier boy
Who grinned at life in empty joy,
Slept soundly through the lonesome dark,
And whistled early with the lark.

In winter trenches, cowed and glum,
With crumps and lice and lack of rum,
He put a bullet through his brain.
No one spoke of him again.

You smug-faced crowds with kindling eye
Who cheer when soldier lads march by,
Sneak home and pray you'll never know
The hell where youth and laughter go.

SIEGFRIED SASSOON

The Send-Off

Down the close darkening lanes they sang their way
To the siding-shed,
And lined the train with faces grimly gay.

Their breasts were stuck all white with wreath and spray
As men's are, dead.

Dull porters watched them, and a casual tramp
Stood staring hard,
Sorry to miss them from the upland camp.

Then, unmoved, signals nodded, and a lamp
Winked to the guard.

So secretly, like wrongs hushed-up, they went.
They were not ours:
We never heard to which front these were sent;

Nor there if they yet mock what women meant
Who gave them flowers.

Shall they return to beating of great bells
In wild train-loads?
A few, a few, too few for drums and yells,

May creep back, silent, to village wells,
Up half-known roads.

WILFRED OWEN

Flying the Flag in Bosnia

Her face is hidden by her hands,
But the hands are enough.
She is slumped by the cross
Which bears her son's name,
Crudely lettered.
An old woman
Whose hair is parted
Straight down the middle.

On one arm of the cross
Some keys and a wallet.
Below, between two lighted candles,
A full cup of coffee,
Left by the grave digger.
Draped on the cross
A shirt, almost new,
Creases still crisp from the iron,
Is unfurled by the wind
Like a flag,
In a country which already has
Too many.

DEREK POWER

Two Fusiliers

And have we done with War at last?
Well, we've been lucky devils both,
And there's no need of pledge or oath
To bind our lovely friendship fast,
By firmer stuff
Close bound enough.

By wire and wood and stake we're bound,
By Fricourt and by Festubert,
By whipping rain, by the sun's glare,
By all the misery and loud sound,
By a Spring day,
By Picard clay.

Show me the two so closely bound
As we, by the wet bond of blood,
By friendship, blossoming from mud,
By Death: we faced him, and we found
Beauty in Death,
In dead men breath.

ROBERT GRAVES

Dulce et Decorum Est

Bent double, like old beggars under sacks,
Knock-kneed, coughing like hags, we cursed through sludge,
Till on the haunting flares we turned our backs
And towards our distant rest began to trudge.
Men marched asleep. Many had lost their boots
But limped on, blood-shod. All went lame; all blind;
Drunk with fatigue; deaf even to the hoots
Of gas shells dropping softly behind.

Gas! GAS! Quick, boys! – An ecstasy of fumbling,
Fitting the clumsy helmets just in time;
But someone still was yelling out and stumbling,
And flound'ring like a man in fire or lime ...
Dim, through the misty panes and thick green light,
As under a green sea, I saw him drowning.

In all my dreams, before my helpless sight,
He plunges at me, guttering, choking, drowning.

If in some smothering dreams you too could pace
Behind the wagon that we flung him in,
And watch the white eyes writhing in his face,
His hanging face, like a devil's sick of sin;
If you could hear, at every jolt, the blood
Come gargling from the froth-corrupted lungs,
Obscene as cancer, bitter as the cud
Of vile, incurable sores on innocent tongues, –
My friend, you would not tell with such high zest
To children ardent for some desperate glory,
The old Lie: Dulce et decorum est
Pro patria mori.

WILFRED OWEN

Dulce et decorum est
Pro patria mori.
It is a sweet and fitting thing
to die for one's country.

Rhodesia

If you had seen
A strong, red pulse
Pump dry a bullet wound
Of darkening blood;
If you had seen
A pallor creep
And drive the sun-gold bloom
From some Rhodesian face;
A clean-limbed boy
Who, laughing died
To keep the spirit of a song,
The child-nostalgia of a poem,
The meaning of a much-loved word,
A way of life
Transcending all invention
Of the human mind;
A dream
Of what he thought was England . . .

. . . Now, in the bitter aftermath,
Perhaps you'd fail
To stem a tear,
And maybe clutch
Some hand as ageing as your own,
Silently,
Remembering in the winter
The many suns that smiled
And did a shining best
And dipped away
Forgotten.

PETER MOULDING

Casualty – Mental Ward

Something has gone wrong inside my head.
The sappers have left mines and wire behind;
I hold long conversations with the dead.

I do not always know what has been said;
The rhythms, not the words, stay in my mind;
Something has gone wrong inside my head.

Not just the sky but grass and trees are red,
The flares and tracers – or I'm colour-blind;
I hold long conversations with the dead.

Their presence comforts and sustains like bread;
When they don't come it's hard to be resigned;
Something has gone wrong inside my head.

They know about the snipers that I dread
And how the world is booby-trapped and mined;
I hold long conversations with the dead;

As all eyes close, they gather round my bed
And whisper consolation. When I find
Something has gone wrong inside my head
I hold long conversations with the dead.

VERNON SCANNELL

Hearing that His Friend was Coming Back from the War

In old days those who went to fight
In three years had one year's leave.
But in *this* war the soldiers are never changed;
They must go on fighting till they die on the battlefield.
I thought of you, so weak and indolent,
Hopelessly trying to learn to march and drill.
That a young man should ever come home again
Seemed about as likely as that the sky should fall.
Since I got the news that you were coming back,
Twice I have mounted to the high wall of your home.
I found your brother mending your horse's stall;
I found your mother sewing your new clothes.
I am half afraid; perhaps it is not true;
Yet I never weary of watching for you on the road.
Each day I go out at the City Gate
With a flask of wine, lest you should come thirsty.
Oh that I could shrink the surface of the World,
So that suddenly I might find you standing at my side!

WANG CHIEN

Translated by Arthur Waley

When I am Dead

When I am dead
Cry for me a little
Think of me sometimes
But not too much.
Think of me now and again
As I was in life
At some moments it's pleasant to recall
But not for long.
Leave me in peace
And I shall leave you in peace
And while you live
Let your thoughts be with the living.

ANON

(traditional Indian)

MCMXIV

Those long uneven lines
Standing as patiently
As if they were stretched outside
The Oval or Villa Park,

The crowns of hats, the sun
On moustached archaic faces
Grinning as if it were all
An August Bank Holiday lark;

And the shut shops, the bleached
Established names on the sunblinds,
The farthings and sovereigns,
And dark-clothed children at play
Called after kings and queens,
The tin advertisements
For cocoa and twist, and the pubs
Wide open all day;

And the countryside not caring;
The place-names all hazed over
With flowering grasses, and fields
Shadowing Domesday lines
Under wheat's restless silence;
The differently-dressed servants
With tiny rooms in huge houses,
The dust behind limousines;

Never such innocence,
Never before or since,
As changed itself to past
Without a word – the men
Leaving the gardens tidy,
The thousands of marriages
Lasting a little while longer:
Never such innocence again.

PHILIP LARKIN

A Motorbike

We had a motorbike all through the war
In an outhouse – thunder, flight, disruption
Cramped in rust, under washing, abashed, outclassed
By the Brens, the Bombs, the Bazookas elsewhere.

The war ended, the explosions stopped.
The men surrendered their weapons
And hung around limply.
Peace took them all prisoner.
They were herded into their home towns.
A horrible privation began
Of working a life up out of the avenues
And the holiday resorts and the dance-halls.

Then the morning bus was as bad as any labour truck,
The foreman, the boss, as bad as the S.S.
And the ends of the street and the bends of the road
And the shallowness of the shops and the shallowness of the beer
And the sameness of the next town
Were as bad as electrified barbed wire.
The shrunk-back war ached in their testicles
And England dwindled to the size of a dog-track.

So there came this quiet young man
And he bought our motorbike for twelve pounds.
And he got it going, with difficulty.
He kicked it into life – it erupted
Out of the six year sleep, and he was delighted.

A week later, astride it, before dawn,
A misty frosty morning,
He escaped

Into a telegraph pole
On the long straight west of Swinton.

TED HUGHES

The General

'Good morning; good morning!' the General said
When we met him last week on our way to the line.
Now the soldiers he smiled at are most of 'em dead,
And we're cursing his staff for incompetent swine.
'He's a cheery old card,' grunted Harry to Jack
As they slogged up to Arras with rifle and pack

.   .   .   .   .

But he did for them both by his plan of attack.

SIEGFRIED SASSOON

The Dying Airman

A handsome young airman lay dying,
And as on the aerodrome he lay,
To the mechanics who round him came sighing,
These last dying words he did say:

'Take the cylinders out of my kidneys,
The connecting-rod out of my brain,
Take the cam-shaft from out of my backbone,
And assemble the engine again.'

ANON

from Bayonet Training

From far away, a mile or so,
The wooden scaffolds could be seen
    On which fat felons swung;
But closer view showed these to be
Sacks, corpulent with straw and tied
    To beams from which they hung.

The sergeant halted his platoon.
'Right lads,' he barked, 'you see them sacks?
    I want you to forget
That sacks is what they are and act
As if they was all Jerries – wait!
    Don't move a muscle yet!

'I'm going to show you how to use
The bayonet as it should be done.
    If any of you feel
Squeamish like, I'll tell you this:
There's one thing Jerry just can't face
    And that thing is cold steel.

'So if we're going to win this war
You've got to understand you must
    Be brutal, ruthless, tough.
I want to hear you scream for blood
As you rip out his guts and see
    The stuff he had for duff.'

The young recruits stood there and watched
And listened as their tutor roared
    And stabbed his lifeless foe;
Their faces were expressionless,
Impassive as the winter skies
    Black with threats of snow.

VERNON SCANNELL

Incubator

The tiny baby sleeps in a cage of wires.
Lights blink on and off:

its legs are thin as matches, and its hair
a fuzz of limpid gold.

Sometimes it arches its tiny body,
stretches itself and yawns,

delicate as an egg in that machinery
which sings its own quiet tune.

Machine, you are my mother now, you feed
with the slow drop of time.

It is warm here, sleepless mother,
raise me to run one day

with my leather schoolbag among blossoms
on a day of lessons and fire.

Wakeful machinery, be good to me,
hear me if I don't breathe,

and ring your alarm bell, the panic
of your kind breast of steel.

Machine, let us sleep together,
on the bosom of the night,

till I grow tall, till I leave you
and seek soft human arms.

IAIN CRICHTON SMITH

Green Beret

He was twelve years old,
and I do not know his name.
The mercenaries took him and his father,
whose name I do not know,
one morning upon the High Plateau.
Green Beret looked down on the frail boy
with the eyes of a hurt animal and thought,
a good fright will make him talk.
He commanded, and the father was taken away
behind the forest's green wall.
'Right kid tell us where they are,
tell us where or your father – dead.'
With eyes now bright and filled with terror
the slight boy said nothing.
'You've got one minute kid', said Green Beret,
'tell us where or we kill father'
and thrust his wrist-watch against a face all eyes,
the second-hand turning, jerking on its way.
'OK boy ten seconds to tell us where they are.'
In the last instant the silver hand shattered the
sky and the forest of trees.
'Kill the old guy' roared Green Beret
and shots hammered out
behind the forest's green wall
and sky and trees and soldiers stood
in silence, and the boy cried out.
Green Beret stood
in silence, as the boy crouched down
and shook with tears,
as children do when their father dies.
'Christ,' said one mercenary to Green Beret,
'he didn't know a damn thing
we killed the old guy for nothing.'
So they all went away,
Green Beret and his mercenaries.

And the boy knew everything.
He knew everything about them, the caves,
the trails, the hidden places and the names,
and in the moment that he cried out,
in that same instant,
protected by frail tears
far stronger than any wall of steel,
they passed everywhere
like tigers
across the High Plateau.

HO THIEN

Children in Wartime

Sirens ripped open
the warm silk of sleep;
we ricocheted to the shelter
moated by streets
that ran with darkness.
People said it was a storm,
but flak
had not the right sound
for rain;
thunder left such huge craters
of silence,
we knew this was no giant
playing bowls.
And later,
when I saw the jaw of glass,
where once had hung
my window spun with stars;
it seemed the sky
lay broken on my floor.

ISOBEL THRILLING

Why the Old Woman Limps

Do you know why the old woman sings?
She is sixty years old with six grandchildren to look after
While her sons and their wives are gone south to dig gold.
Each day she milks the goat, sells the milk to buy soap,
Feeds and washes the children, and tethers the goat.
In the evening she tells all stories of old at the fireside:
I know why the old woman sings.

Do you know when the old woman sleeps?
She rests with the dark, at night she thinks of
Tomorrow: she's to feed the children and graze the goat.
She's to weed the garden, water the seedling beans,
The thatch has to be mended, the barnyard cleared.
Maize pounded, chaff winnowed, millet ground, fire lit . . .
I do not know when the old woman sleeps.

Do you know why the old woman limps?
She goes to fetch water in the morning
        and the well is five miles away,
Goes to fetch firewood with her axe
        and the forest is five miles the other way,
Goes to the fields to look for pumpkin leaves
        leaving the goat tethered to the well tree
And hurries home to the children to cook:
I know why the old woman limps.

LUPENGA MPHANDE

Waiting for Thelma's Laughter

for Thelma, my West Indian born Afro-American neighbour

You wanna take the world
in hand
and fix-it-up
the way you fix your living room

You wanna reach out and crush
life's big and small injustices
in the fire and honey
of your hands

You wanna scream
cause your head's too small
for your dreams

and the children
running round
acting like lil clowns
breaking the furniture down

while I sit through
it all watching you
knowing any time now
your laughter's gonna come

to drown and heal us all

GRACE NICHOLS

deconstruction ...

of ¢v¢ryon¢ ¢ls¢'s id¢as
of r¢lationships
of som¢one ¢ls¢'s ¢go

just kp th structur

somthing for rconstruction
misconcption   misconstruction
dstruction

ncessity is th mothr of invntion

govrnmnts of dconstruction
by mony   rcession

go to work
collct rdundancy

mov from th manor   statly hom
to th convrtd stabl block
sll th antiqu furnitur   silvr
manag without hating
            "   "   phon
                    "   tv
                            ovn
chapst food is ric and lntils
swlld by watr rats

go bankrupt
into tmporary accommodation
car nds watr vry fw yards
drivs on thr gars   grinds to a halt
travl by bus

can't afford cinma   pub
        "   "   cloths
                "   shos
                        food

crim rat up
3 gnrations unmploymnt
ric and lntils

dconstruct thir vido
thiv thir bmw
        " cd playr
nick thir cashpoint card
no mor ric and lntils

ya though I spak
with th tongus of mn
or of angls   of building socitis
of banks   of advrtizrs and
insuranc agnts
yt hav not mony

I am nothing

TILLA BRADING

The Bicycle Ride

I step into the Autumn morning
like a First Communicant
and ride off down the lane,
singing.
Across the frosty fields
someone is mending fences
knock knock knock,
and a twig that's caught
in my bicycle spokes
tinkles like a musical box.
The village smells of wood-ash
and warm horses.
Shining crows rise
into the sky like hymns.

I have to pass the church
where my father was buried.

It's a wonderful church.
The Christ in the chancel
is carved by Eric Gill.
There are guidebooks in the nave,
and every day the villagers come
to put fresh flowers
on the graves. My father's
is under the yew tree
by the wall. I look at it
out of the corner of my eye
as I go cycling past,
making for open country.

We didn't go this way
after the funeral –
my mother and me,
and my sad unfamiliar aunts
crying and crying
for their lost brother.
In hired cars,
we went straight home,
where some kind person
had made us tea
and tiny sandwiches.
They were like pocket-handkerchiefs.
Pat, pat, pat ... My father
used to dry my tears like that.

SELIMA HILL

'Maurice'

I never shall love the snow again
    Since Maurice died:
With corniced drift it blocked the lane,
And sheeted in a desolate plain
    The country side.

The trees with silvery rime bedight
    Their branches bare.
By day no sun appeared; by night
The hidden moon shed thievish light
    In the misty air.

We fed the birds that flew around
    In flocks to be fed:
No shelter in holly or brake they found.
The speckled thrush on the frozen ground
    Lay frozen and dead.

We skated on stream and pond; we cut
    The crinching snow
To Doric temple or Arctic hut;
We laughed and sang at nightfall, shut
    By the fireside glow.

Yet grudged we our keen delights before
    Maurice should come.
We said, In-door or out-of-door
We shall love life for a month or more,
    When he is home.

They brought him home; 'twas two days late
    For Christmas day:
Wrapped in white, in solemn state,
A flower in his hand, all still and straight
    Our Maurice lay.

And two days ere the year outgave
    We laid him low.
The best of us truly were not brave,
When we laid Maurice down in his grave
    Under the snow.

ROBERT BRIDGES

Thoughts After Visiting Westminster City Council's Archives

I wonder what befell
Louisa Dell?
Her eight years tucked inside her head,
Both parents dead.
Could God not find it in his head to pardon
This orphan of St Paul's in Covent Garden?
The parish that had saved her as a child
Meek and milk,
For the sum of four pounds and one shilling
Sold her as willing
And obedient.
So to the north she went,
And in a factory there they were to show
Her how to print on calico.
At eight years old she was thus committed,
Alone, but for her eight years, she submitted.
For could God bother with one child
Or any,
When she was only one
Among so many?

And who are we to castigate his pride
Who take the battered babies in our stride?
Each year, they tell us, cruelty increases.
We take long leases
On the joys with which we're blest.
Forget the rest.
Young things still suffer, live small lives in hell,
As long ago did one Louisa Dell.

KAY HARGREAVES

Tich Miller

Tich Miller wore glasses
with elastoplast-pink frames
and had one foot three sizes larger than the other.

When they picked teams for outdoor games
she and I were always the last two
left standing by the wire-mesh fence.

We avoided one another's eyes,
stooping, perhaps, to re-tie a shoelace,
or affecting interest in the flight

of some fortunate bird, and pretended
not to hear the urgent conference:
'Have Tubby!' 'No, no, have Tich!'

Usually they chose me, the lesser dud,
and she lolloped, unselected,
to the back of the other team.

At eleven we went to different schools.
In time I learned to get my own back,
sneering at hockey-players who couldn't spell.

Tich died when she was twelve.

WENDY COPE

You Will Forget

If you stay in comfort too long
you will not know
the weight of a water pot
on the bald head of the village woman

You will forget
the weight of three bundles of thatch grass
on the sinewy neck of the woman
whose baby cries on her back
for a blade of grass in its eyes

Sure, if you stay in comfort too long
you will not know the pain
of child birth without a nurse in white

You will forget
the thirst, the cracked dusty lips
of the woman in the valley
on her way to the headman who isn't there

You will forget
the pouring pain of a thorn prick
with a load on the head.
If you stay in comfort too long

You will forget
the wailing in the valley
of women losing a husband in the mines.

You will forget
the rough handshake of coarse palms
full of teary sorrow at the funeral.

If you stay in comfort too long
You will not hear
the shrieky voice of old warriors sing
the songs of fresh stored battlefields.

You will forget
the unfeeling bare feet
gripping the warm soil turned by the plough

You will forget
the voice of the season talking to the oxen.

CHENJERAI HOVE

The Bustle in a House

The Bustle in a House
The Morning after Death
Is solemnest of industries
Enacted upon earth –

The Sweeping up the Heart,
And putting Love away
We shall not want to use again
Until Eternity.

EMILY DICKINSON

Requiescat

Strew on her roses, roses,
    And never a spray of yew!
In quiet she reposes;
    Ah, would that I did too.

Her mirth the world required;
    She bathed it in smiles of glee,
But her heart was tired, tired,
    And now they let her be.

Her life was turning, turning,
    In mazes of heat and sound.
But for peace her soul was yearning,
    And now peace laps her round.

Her cabin'd, ample spirit,
    It flutter'd and fail'd for breath.
To-night it doth inherit
    The vasty hall of death.

MATTHEW ARNOLD

People

Some people talk and talk
and never say a thing.
Some people look at you
and birds begin to sing.

Some people laugh and laugh
and yet you want to cry.
Some people touch your hand
and music fills the sky.

CHARLOTTE ZOLOTOW

Fleur Adcock, who was born in New Zealand but now lives in London, started writing when she was six. She lived in England for eight years as a young girl and changed schools eleven times in that period. She feels that being an outsider has sharpened her powers of observation.

Anna Akhmatova was born in 1889 in Russia and published her first poetry in 1907. She was a prolific writer but her later work was suppressed under Stalin. She died in 1966 after being recognised as a great poet in the Western world.

Simon Armitage, poet, part-time probation officer and literary editor, writes about everyday life, including both weird and ordinary people, with humour and perception. Try his collections *Zoom, Kid,* and *Book of Matches.*

Matthew Arnold, who died in 1888, was a schools inspector for thirty-five years. As he travelled the country, he observed poor social conditions and the decline in religious faith, both of which contributed to the loneliness depicted in 'To Marguerite'. The longer poems 'The Forsaken Merman' and 'Sohrab and Rustum', are worth looking for.

Margaret Atwood is a highly acclaimed Canadian poet and novelist.

Chris Banks first published 'The Gift' in *Rialto;* it also appears in the writer's first collection, *Watching the Home Movies.* It describes a true incident in her family life.

Patricia Beer grew up in Devon and uses a West Country background for many of her poems, though 'Pigeons' could, in fact, be set outside any suitable church you can picture.

James Berry was born in Jamaica and came to London when he was twenty-four. He has worked widely in multicultural education and published a great many poems including the collections *Fractured Circles* and *Lucy's Letter and Loving.*

Sujata Bhatt grew up in India and Canada but now lives in Germany. You feel no doubt as you read the poems in this anthology that the poet is drawing on memories of her past.

William Blake (1757–1827) was an engraver and painter as well as a poet with a mystic vision.

Tilla Brading, who is interested in all forms of poetry, including staging performance poetry and co-editing a magazine, experiments frequently in her own writing.

Robert Bridges (1844–1930) became Poet Laureate in 1913 and was one of the founders of the Society for Pure English. He was a very popular writer in his day, though is not so widely read now.

Edwin Brock writes compassionate, questioning poetry. His poem 'Five Ways to Kill a Man' is one of the most widely anthologised poems of recent years.

Rupert Brooke, born in 1887, was already a successful poet when he went to war in 1914. His war sonnets, including 'The Soldier', published early in 1915, were widely read and stirred up patriotic fervour, encouraging other young men to enlist and fight for their country. Rupert Brooke died of blood poisoning at the end of 1915. It was left to others such as Wilfred Owen to depict war – the darker side, in his case.

Martin Carter, a Guyanan poet, first came to fame with his *Poems of Resistance* published in 1954, based on his experience in fighting colonialism. He is now writing in more peaceful times.

Geoffrey Chaucer was born about 1340 and lived until 1400. His famous *Canterbury Tales* were printed by Caxton's press. (This was the first printing press in England and marked the beginning of the mass-circulation of the written word.) Chanticleer features in 'The Nun's Priest's Tale', one of the Canterbury Tales which a group of pilgrims told to each other to while away the time on a pilgrimage from London to Canterbury.

Frank Chipasula, who has long been a political exile from Malawi, writes about his home country, about friends in prison and betrayal. In 'Ars Poetica' he expresses his determination to stick by his principles and not to compromise.

John Clare (1793–1864) was the son of a farm labourer, an unusual background for a poet at that time. He popularised rural themes in poetry, writing with sincerity about the countryside and the working people around him. The latter part of his life was spent in a lunatic asylum from where he published some of his best work, in spite of suffering from depression and the recurrent delusion that he was a prize-fighter.

Gillian Clarke has lived in South Wales most of her life and is a poetry editor and teacher as well as a poet.

Wendy Cope has become best known as a humorous poet and for 'sending up' or parodying other writers.

Frances Cornford (1886–1960) was born in Cambridge where she spent most of her life. Her *Collected Poems* appeared in 1954.

Angela Costen is a versatile poet and teacher.

Iain Crichton Smith – born on the Isle of Lewis in the Outer Hebrides, Crichton Smith is both a poet and a short-story writer. His work shows how local detail and universal themes can be powerfully combined.

Peter Dale, a truthful and exacting writer, has taught and written about poetry, as well as co-editing the poetry magazine *Agenda*.

Emily Dickinson (1830–86) was an American poet, born in Massachusetts. She became a recluse in her mid-twenties and inhabited a private world. Only seven of her two thousand poems are known to have been published in her lifetime. Once considered an eccentric minor poet, she is now looked on as an important and original writer.

H. D. (Hilda Doolittle) was an American poet (1888–1961) who became a leader of the 'Imagist' movement in poetry, with her sharp, spare use of images being widely copied. In 'Sheltered Garden', H. D. expresses the feeling of her life and freedom being smothered, like 'pears wadded in cloth'.

Lord Alfred Douglas (1870–1934) – a minor poet, friend of Oscar Wilde.

Helen Dunmore is a novelist and poet. Her collection *Raw Garden* explores the impact of people on the landscape, though the climate is the stronger force in 'Permafrost', in this anthology. 'In the Desert Knowing Nothing' is a sympathetic response to a bewildering situation.

Paul Durcan is a popular Irish poet, writing with humour and irony both on Irish themes and on the general human condition.

Robert Etty – I came across 'Special Green' in *Odyssey*, a poetry magazine, and it seemed appropriate for 'Bone and Stone'. Robert Etty's most recent collection is called *Marking Places*.

U. A. Fanthorpe – Ursula Fanthorpe – taught English for sixteen years until, in order to have time for writing, she became, in her own words, 'a middle-aged drop-out'. She has now published several collections of poems. 'Not My Best Side' comes to life if you think of the St George and the Dragon story, or, better still, study Uccello's painting of that famous encounter.

Linda France began to make her name as a poet when she appeared in *New Women Poets* in 1990. She has also won poetry prizes.

Wilfred Gibson (1878–1958) had no formal education but published his first poems in 1902. Like Rupert Brooke he fought in the First World War, but, unlike his friend, he survived to lament the dead.

Sheila Glen Bishop, an artist as a young woman, started writing poetry later in life, and draws on a wide range of personal experiences.

Robert Graves (1895–1985) was a distinguished poet, novelist and critic. He fought in the First World War and was a friend of Siegfried Sassoon and Wilfred Owen (see 'Life and Death'). His war experiences are vividly recalled in *Goodbye To All That*, a biography.

Thomas Hardy, born in Dorset in 1840, wrote widely about the West of England and is best known for his novels, several of which have been made into popular films, such as *Tess of the D'Urbervilles* and *Far from the Madding Crowd*. But Hardy always considered his fiction as inferior to his poetry. He died in 1928.

Kay Hargreaves was inspired to write about Louisa Dell by the episode described in the title. She writes to record and explore events, and does not usually seek publication.

Tony Harrison is a poet and translator. His childhood and family life provide much of the material for his poetry.

John Hawkhead is widely published in poetry magazines in Britain and America. 'You Were Saying?' was a joint effort with his wife Patricia.

Seamus Heaney, who was born in the north of Ireland but now lives in the Republic, often draws on his rural childhood in his poems, as in 'Follower'. He conveys ideas through precise physical observations and is a powerful user of words and rhythm. In the early nineties he was Professor of Poetry at Oxford.

Selima Hill says that she became a writer because she was lonely as a child. But she discovered that writing was a beast as well as a friend, 'a black, shaggy, misshapen animal' that wouldn't leave her alone. Many of her poems have a sharp humour.

Gerard Manley Hopkins (1844–89) ignored most of the conventions of poetry and forced words and expressions into the form that most closely expressed his emotions. When he decided to become a Jesuit priest, in 1868, he destroyed most of his writing and after this only wrote on what he considered to be suitable subjects, such as beauty and religion, which he saw as bound together. He was a friend of Robert Bridges whose 'Hill Pines' shares a theme with 'Binsey Poplars'.

A. E. Housman (1859–1936) was a poet and Latin scholar and wrote in a clear, simple style. His *A Shropshire Lad*, three small volumes of poems published in 1896, was slow to sell but later became very popular.

Chenjerai Hove, who is now a journalist in Harare, was involved in his country's fight for independence. In 'You Will Forget' he is writing about friends who 'sold out' on the poor from the villages once they had achieved an easy life for themselves.

Ted Hughes, Poet Laureate since 1984, was brought up in Yorkshire. He draws on the background of a harsh climate and farming in many of his poems but he is always experimenting in new directions and defies classification. He has written several books of children's verse.

Victor Hugo (1802–85) was a French poet, dramatist and novelist.

John Nangoza Jebe was shot by police in a Good Friday procession in Port Elizabeth, South Africa in 1956. This poem, 'For a Dead African', now speaks for him.

Elizabeth Jennings worked in a library and in advertising whilst publishing her first collection of poetry: *Poems* (1953). Her *Collected Poems* were published in 1967.

Ben Jonson (1572–1637) was a dramatist and poet writing at the same time as Shakespeare. In fact, Shakespeare acted in one of Jonson's plays, 'Everyman in his Humour', in 1598.

Sylvia Kantaris lives in Cornwall by the sea. 'Snapshotland' comes from her collection *The Sea at my Door*.

John Keats, born in 1795, trained to be a surgeon but gave up this career for poetry. He wrote 'La Belle Dame sans Merci' in 1819, the year in which he became engaged to Fanny Brawne, the love of his life. Sore throats, the first sign of his tuberculosis, began to plague him, but he wrote steadily on, his reputation slowly growing. He set off for Italy for his health in 1820 but died in Rome in February. He is now considered one of the greatest poets of the nineteenth century.

Philip Larkin, who died in 1985, was one of the most popular poets of this century but he was a retiring man, known affectionately by his friends as the 'hermit of Hull'.

Michael Laskey – 'Registers' comes from a collection of his poems published in 1991, in which he writes of family and everyday matters, including the experience of raising his sons.

D. H. (David Herbert) Lawrence (1885–1930) was a poet and novelist, but more widely known for his novels, which include *Sons and Lovers,* and *Lady Chatterley's Lover.*

Jonathan Lloyd – 'Murdered Lovers' Bodies', on an episode from the war in Bosnia, comes from an anthology called *Headlines in Verse*, containing a real news story in each poem.

Liz Lochhead first started writing poetry at nineteen, when she was an art student, after having 'quite a strong distaste' for poetry at school. Many of her poems are intended for speaking aloud – some in Scottish dialect – and she gives poetry readings all over the country.

Norman MacCaig was born and educated in Edinburgh. Much of his poetry is influenced by his Scottish background, though he writes for a universal audience.

Patricia McCarthy's first poetry book was published in America and her second collection in England. In her poetry she often draws on mythology and on her experiences of life in several continents. She writes in a strongly personal, disciplined style.

Louis MacNeice (1907–63) – though educated in England, MacNeice was born in Belfast and retained, in his verse, the Irish lyricism and rhythms of his childhood. He was also a writer of radio documentaries and plays.

Andrew Marvell (1621–78) – much of his poetry was satirical and political. He wrote several poems in Cromwell's honour and, after the Restoration, from his position as a Member of Parliament, wrote pamphlets attacking the government.

Charlotte Mew (1869–1928) struggled to keep writing her powerful and passionate poetry against a background of poverty, ill-health and depression. Her reputation has grown steadily since her death.

Elma Mitchell has lived in England all her adult life but was born and brought up in Scotland. Her poetry, firmly fixed on people, has an inimitable warmth and humour.

Andrew Motion has a considerable reputation as both poet and literary critic.

Peter Moulding, who saw active service in the RAF in the Second World War, wrote this poem from a personal knowledge of Africa and of warfare.

Lupenga Mphande, an exile from Malawi, now teaches at an American university.

Grace Nichols, from Guyana, but now living in England, brings the vibrance and resilience of her background to her poetry.

Frank Ormsby, a Northern Irish poet, is barely represented by the short poem 'Under the Stairs', but the last line – 'a store of candles ...', gives the title to an interesting collection of his work.

Wilfred Owen was the First World War poet most responsible for drawing public attention to the appalling suffering inflicted by war in the name of patriotism. He was born in 1893 and was killed in France in 1918, a week before the Armistice. Most of his famous poems were written in the year before his death.

Brian Patten was one of the Liverpool Poets with Adrian Henri and Roger McGough. His poetry readings around the country in theatres and schools are tremendously popular.

Sylvia Plath was born in Boston, America, in 1932. Her poetry is highly personal and hauntingly vivid. She suffered from depression and took her life in 1963. Her *Collected Poems* were published in 1981 with the co-operation of her husband Ted Hughes.

Derek Power – a pharmacist by profession, Derek Power writes sparingly and precisely, as if looking through a lens at other people's lives. His Bosnian poem first appeared in *The Independent*.

Christina Rossetti (1830–94) was a sensitive, frustrated poet, trapped in the restricted female world of her time. But the innovative skill of her poetry, the short, irregularly rhymed lines, contributed to the next generation's freer style of writing.

Edna St Vincent Millay (1892–1950) was an American poet born in Maine. Her reckless, romantic personality brought early popularity to her poetry in the twenties, but she is not so widely read today as she is no longer dangerously modern.

Siegfried Sassoon (1886–1967) – his best poetry was written in the trenches in the First World War. Whilst in hospital, shell-shocked, he met Wilfred Owen and encouraged the younger man's writing. They shared a hatred of patriotic cant and viewed the war leaders with contempt, as 'The General' shows.

Vernon Scannell shows an awareness of the darker side of life in his poetry, as well as the predictable and domestic. He has published several collections.

William Shakespeare (1564–1616) – dramatist, actor and poet: his *Collected Works* are reputedly second only to the Bible in the world best-seller stakes.

Wole Soyinka, born in Nigeria, is a dramatist, novelist and poet with a worldwide reputation.

Lord Alfred Tennyson (1809–92) was a prolific and popular writer. He was appointed Poet Laureate in 1850, in succession to Wordsworth.

Charles Tennyson Turner (1808–79) was older brother to the more famous Alfred.

A. S. J. Tessimond was an enigmatic and interesting poet who captured the spirit of the ordinary person in different urban situations: the businessman in the bowler hat, the man in the saloon bar or the dance hall, the romantic, the hypochondriac, and so on.

Ho Thien, a Vietnamese writer, focuses in 'Green Beret' on the treachery of war and individual courage.

Edward Thomas (1878–1917) was killed in the First World War and most of his poems were published posthumously. He is not known primarily as a war poet but as a loving observer of the English countryside.

R. S. Thomas (Ronald Stuart Thomas) was born in Cardiff in 1913. He became a clergyman and his writing is influenced by his work among rural communities in a bleak landscape.

Isobel Thrilling, who was brought up in North Yorkshire, has had poetry broadcast on Yorkshire Television and on BBC radio. She has won several prizes for her poetry.

Derek Walcott is a Caribbean poet with a large and powerful output, mainly centred around the islands, their history and his mixed ancestry. He teaches at Boston University. He won the Nobel Prize for literature in 1992.

Alice Walker, poet, novelist and critic, was born in Georgia, America and now lives in San Francisco. She has won a number of awards for her writing.

Wang Chien (AD 756–835), a Chinese poet of the T'ang dynasty.

Paul D. Wapshott served in a parachute regiment.

Hugo Williams, son of an actor, moved around a great deal during his childhood, which he has written widely about. His dilemma when composing his 'letter home' in 'At Least a Hundred Words' amusingly captures boarding-school life.

W. B. Yeats (William Butler Yeats, 1865–1939) was born in Dublin but educated in England. 'An Irish Airman …' is not a typical sample of Yeats' poetry, yet it conveys the haunting quality of his work. Much of Yeats' writing, which includes plays, was preoccupied with Irish folklore and legends. He helped to create a National Theatre in Ireland.

Charlotte Zolotow, an American, is the author of more than fifty books for young children, besides writing poetry.

What is poetry for? Why do people write it?

Writing poetry is a way of expressing ideas and emotions, or of recording a special event. The writer's purpose is usually to communicate with other people but sometimes a poet writes to sort out her/his own thoughts.

Browse through this book at random, or section by section; pause when you find a poem that you like; read it through again – out loud, if possible. Ask yourself, 'Why do I like this poem?' and 'What's it about?'

Although the subject matter is important in a poem – as in all forms of writing – poetry has a special quality that enables atmosphere and mood to be passed on by the poet to the reader (hinting, perhaps, at things not fully expressed). When you ask yourself what a poem is about, you should probe beyond the obvious story of the poem and ask further questions about the poet's feelings and your response.

Below are some guidelines to help you to focus on the poems and to explore and enjoy them more fully.

Why do you like a poem?

Is your reason for liking a poem because it:
- makes you laugh?
- tells a good story?
- makes you feel sad, loving, tender?
- reminds you of something in your own life?

Or do you like it for some other reason?

What's the poem about?

- Who is speaking in the poem?
- To whom?
- What about? (Remember that it may be about several things.)
- What does the poet feel, and what do you feel? (This is the **mood** of the poem.)
- How are the ideas being expressed?

You will have an opinion on the first four questions after a close reading of the poem and discussing it with other people. There may be several different, well-supported points of view; all of them deserve consideration.

The fifth question, 'How are the ideas being expressed?' will be more easily answered using the following guidelines.

What to look for

Language – choosing words

Since poetry is a means of expressing ideas and emotions in a concise and vivid way, every word is (or should be) chosen with care. Remember that the poet is thinking about sound as well as about meaning as s/he selects words. Study the poet's choice of words as you read each poem, and see how words are used. Be aware of the following:

Context: key words used in a particular position in a line to maximise their impact.
Double meanings, which may lurk behind words and phrases.
Repetition of words and phrases. Is repetition being used for emphasis of meaning or to contribute to atmosphere and rhythm?
The **music** or **rhythm** of each line depends on the choice and placing of words. Rhythm, working alongside the meaning of words, helps to shape the whole poem. A fast rhythm can make words exciting or angry. A slow rhythm may emphasise thoughtfulness or peace. But not always.

Ask yourself why the poet has used a particular form. What effect is s/he trying to achieve? Has s/he succeeded?

This example from 'Binsey Poplars' (page 62) shows how Gerard Manley Hopkins made words work for him:

> All felled, felled, are all felled;
> Of a fresh and following folded rank
> Not spared, not one
> That dandled a sandalled
> Shadow that swam or sank.

The repetition of 'felled' suggests a person in shock, repeating something s/he does not quite believe in. There is further repetition in the letter *f* carried through to the second line to emphasise key words. Repetition of an initial letter is called **alliteration**.

There is also an echo of syllables in 'dandled' and 'sandalled', as Hopkins mourns the lost line of trees, and their vanished reflection from the water. This rhyming within a line is called **internal rhyme**.

In the last line the *s* and *a* sound in 'shadow', 'swam' and 'sank' leaves the words lingering in the reader's mind. Sound repetition is called **assonance**.

'Folded rank' makes me think of soldiers being cut down in battle, but it might suggest a different image to someone else.

Images

Images or **word pictures** are a way of creating atmosphere or illustrating ideas. One form of word picture is achieved by using **comparisons**. When the poet surprises you by comparing unlikely things, it helps you to form a memorable picture in your mind. Hopkins (above) gives us the idea of reflected twigs being like the straps of a sandal.

Similes

Sometimes the comparison is a **simile**, simply stating that an object or an idea is *like* something else, for example: 'A nice warm sloppy tilting belly ... *Like* a bowl of porridge'; or 'Tangy *as* blackberries, luscious *as* avocado' ('People Etcetera', Elma Mitchell page 82).

In Seamus Heaney's poem 'Follower' (page 89) there is a strong visual picture of the poet's father ploughing:

> His shoulders globed *like* a full sail strung
> Between the shafts and the furrow.

The words 'like' and 'as' will help you to pick out similes.

Metaphors

In the same lines of Seamus Heaney quoted above you can find another figure of speech, a **metaphor**, where a comparison or likeness is implied rather than stated directly. In the words, 'His shoulders globed', Heaney uses a globe as a metaphor to suggest that his father's shoulders were both solid and rounded.

There is also a metaphor of the sea that runs through the poem, with the idea, rather than an explicit statement, that the ploughed field is the ocean. After the sail image in the first verse, you are told the 'sod rolled over without breaking' which gives the suggestion of a wave; and the use of 'wake' in verse four, followed by 'dipping and rising', all add to the sea images and strengthen the whole visual picture created by the metaphor.

In 'To Marguerite' (page 78) there is a long metaphor (or extended metaphor) running through the poem, in which individuals are seen as lonely islands, originating in the same land mass, now cut off in the sea of life.

> Oh! then a longing like despair
> Is to their farthest caverns sent;
> For surely once, they feel, we were
> Parts of a single continent!
> Now round us spreads the watery plain –
> Oh might our marges meet again!

The fact that the islands are given human qualities such as despair and longing, adds to the pathos of the poem. This giving of human qualities to objects or animals is called **personification**.

For further short, sharp metaphors look at 'Children in Wartime' (Isobel Thrilling page 113):

> Sirens ripped open
> the warm silk of sleep;
> we ricocheted to the shelter
> moated by streets

In these opening lines images of savage tearing and noise, followed by violent movement, are contrasted with safe, warm sleep. There is also the hint of parachutes in 'silk', and guns as well as sleepy stumbling about in 'ricocheted'.

Read on and pick out more metaphors in this poem. Think about them and discuss them. The images conjured up by the metaphors may not be the same for everybody.

As you get used to looking closely at poems you will become aware of all kinds of images and half-images, formed both by direct comparisons and the merest suggestions. You do not necessarily need to identify the images by name to enjoy their impact but it is useful to your own writing to think about how their effect is achieved.

Form or structure

A quick glance at how a poem is set out on a page will tell you something about form. As you look through the pages of this book, you will notice:
- poems with verses (or stanzas) of equal length
- verses of irregular length
- lines in a single group
- lines of varying length
- end-stopped lines, which finish or pause before the next line
- some poems which rhyme, others with irregular or no rhyme
- poems written in sentences, obeying the rules of grammar
- poems using words more randomly, with no punctuation or capital letters.

In general, people writing poetry today will use the form that they feel best suits each poem and adds the greatest impact to it. Probing and questioning may lead a poet to a loose, open style, whereas deeply held views and tight emotions might best be contained within a formal pattern. But not necessarily. There is no right and wrong style for a particular situation.

However, well into the twentieth century there were accepted conventions and styles to poetry, partly depending on subject matter, which influenced poetry writing. Some poets still prefer to work within a tight framework of rules. For example, 'The Rose' by Peter Dale, a contemporary poet (page 84), is based on the Petrarchan sonnet, a fourteen-line verse form, popular four hundred years ago.

There are several types of verse and line forms:
- traditional pattern: lines of equal length, often broken into regular verses but sometimes in a block, as in 'To His Coy Mistress' (page 88)
- a repetitive rhythm
- a regular rhyming scheme
- blank verse, which has no rhyme but relies on a strong rhythm.

Rhythm or metre

In traditional or formal verse, each line has a set number of beats with a rhythm that can be tapped out like a tune. This is known as the **metre** and it is used in various ways for special effects, as it is in music. A popular form of metre is made up of a short beat, or stress, followed by a long one (known together as the **iambus**), as in Lord Tennyson's 'The Brook' (page 53):

> I wind about, and in and out,
> With here a blossom sailing,
> And here and there a lusty trout,
> And here and there a grayling.

Here you can count four short + long beats in the first and third lines, with three short + long beats and an extra short beat in the other two lines, which gives variety to the verse but still forms a pattern.

Shakespeare was particularly fond of lines with five double beats (the **iambic pentameter**), as in the sonnet on page 81:

> Shall I compare thee to a summer's day?
> Thou art more lovely and more temperate:
> Rough winds do shake the darling buds of May,
> And summer's lease hath all too short a date:

> ˅ = a short beat
> — = a long beat

In this century, strongly influenced by such poets as Gerard Manley Hopkins and Christina Rossetti, the rhythm in a poem is often close to the rhythm of everyday speech – see, for example, 'Song of the Battery Hen', by Edwin Brock, on page 50:

> We can't grumble about accommodation:
> we have a new concrete floor that's
> always dry, four wall that are
> painted white, and a sheet-iron roof

But this is only one of many types of verse being written today.

Rhyme

Rhymes are made when words, or parts of words, that are placed close together, sound the same, for example sun/bun, long/song, consider/remember – but *not* though/plough. **Half-rhymes** are: caught/coat, flash/flush, poet/work.

A study of the rhymes at the end of the lines in 'First Love' by John Clare (page 77) will show you their sequence: 'hour' rhymes with 'flower', and 'sweet' with 'complete'. You can indicate this with *a b a b*:

I ne'er was struck before that hour   *a*
    With love so sudden and so sweet.   *b*
Her face it bloomed like a sweet flower   *a*
    And stole my heart away complete.   *b*

You can now use *c d* to denote the new rhymes through the poem and discover the overall rhyming pattern.

- Is the rhyming scheme consistent?
- Do you think it suits the subject of the poem?

Free verse

What we know as free verse started as a breaking away from the restraints of formal verse. It isn't necessarily as unrestricted as it sounds but the poet can choose his or her own form to suit the subject matter and to give his or her own special imprint to a poem. S/he will often use verses like paragraphs, or place a word strategically for a particular emphasis.

This example is from 'Anniversaries: The Fourth' by Andrew Motion on page 80:

Anniversary weather: I drive
under a raw sunset, the road
cramped between drifts, hedges
polished into sharp crests.

The placing of 'I drive', 'the road' and 'hedges' at the ends of lines, in an unusual position, encourages the reader to emphasise these words. If you read the verse out loud with 'I drive' at the beginning of the second line, 'the road' at the beginning of the third, and 'hedges' starting the fourth, you will not know which words to stress.

Some poets explore completely new forms of layout. **Concrete** or **shape** poems, for instance, have a strong dependence on the way words and lines are set out on the page, sometimes in the shape of an animal or a fruit. 'You Were Saying' (Patricia and John Hawkhead, page 87) incorporates a shopping list into expressing the relationship of a couple shopping together. The poem needs to be seen on the page to be fully appreciated. Tilla Brading in 'deconstruction …' (page 116) breaks up words by removing one vital letter, to express a person's life coming apart; but the same writer uses a totally different style in 'Nativity Play' (page 6) to depict a disgruntled teenager.

Teach yourself to be conscious, as you read poetry, of the way poems have been crafted. Try out different forms of writing for yourself.

There is nothing sacred about poetry.

These questions and activities have been devised for the purpose of sharpening your observation and strengthening your skills in talking about, or 'criticising', a poem. Remember to refer back to the *Focus* section on pages 135–40.

All the skills that you use in answering these questions will help you to tackle 'unseen' poems in an examination.

It is important to support your points in your answer with quotations, which can be whole lines, or just one or two words. Always quote examples from the text when writing about a poem, even if you are not specifically asked to do so. (Set out the separate lines of the poem for longer quotations, and use quotation marks/speech marks.)

It would be valuable to discuss some of these questions in pairs or groups before writing anything down. (Remember Elma Mitchell's warning against tackling 'dangerous poems' by yourself – page 28.)

However, despite Elma Mitchell's (ironic) warning, you will *not* be expected to have a definitive answer to everything. It is quite acceptable – and sometimes good policy – to say: 'I think the poet means' or 'S/he seems to be saying', and so on. Show that you are exploring the poem and are open-minded.

1   'Telephone Conversation', page 10. Write about this poem and its effect on you. Show how the writer brings out the contrasting characters of the two people on the phone. Use quotations to support your points.

2   'A Motorbike', page 108. What picture does this poem give you of the war and the time after the war? Pick out words and lines that illustrate your points. What do you feel is Hughes' attitude towards 'the quiet young man'? Give reasons for your answer.

3   Study 'Kankaria Lake', page 72.
    (a) Describe what is happening, and the boy's thoughts and feelings.
    (b) What is the mood or atmosphere of the poem? Which lines in particular build up this atmosphere for you, and how do these lines achieve their effect?

4   *One Another*, pages 75–96. Find two or three poems in this section, each dealing with different relationships, and compare both the themes and the way in which the poets write about their subject. What is your response to each poem? (You will probably find it easier if you start by writing about each poem separately.)

5   'The Man in the Bowler Hat' and 'One', pages 2 and 13. Write your response to each of these poems, individually; then say which you prefer, and why. Quote and discuss lines that you like.

6 'Not My Best Side', page 46. What is this poem about? (See 'Poets in this anthology', page 127.) Pick out humorous features in each section and comment on them. How much truth, in your opinion, lies behind the humour?

7 'A Far Cry from Africa', page 7. In this poem Derek Walcott is wrestling with his thoughts. Write down in detail the theme of the poem using quotations to show the poet's mood and the strength of his feelings. Do you think it is a successful poem? Give reasons for your opinion.

8 'People Etcetera', page 82.
(a) What do you think the poet's attitude is towards people in general? Back up your opinion.
(b) Pick out some of the comparisons that you like and say why you like them.
(c) How does Elma Mitchell give shape and emphasis to this poem?
(d) Write a similar poem of your own using 'Dogs are … Cats are … Parents are … Teachers are …', for example.

9 Select two war poems and compare them, showing both the similarities and the difference in attitude and style of the poets.

10 Bone and Stone, pages 49–74. Choose two or more poems from this section, on a similar theme (for example Wildlife, Trees, Environment). Say what each poem is about and what your personal response to it is. Use short quotations to illustrate your points. Which poem do you prefer, and why?

11 'The White Tiger' and 'Mountain Lion', pages 57 and 64. These two poems seem to share a point of view. What is it? To what extent does each poet succeed in making you sympathize with his feelings? Quote lines that you find particularly powerful and comment on any other points that interest you.

12 Look at two or three different types of media presented in the Media Media section (pages 25–48). Describe the poems and your response to them. Quote and comment on effective lines.

13 Choose two or three poems from the Strictly Personal section (pages 1–24) that have a sad or thoughtful mood, and compare the themes. How does each writer present his/her subject? Quote to support your points.

14 Look at 'Campsite: Maentwrog' page 11 and 'A Holiday' by Margaret Atwood, page 70.
(a) In what way are the campers 'practising our characteristic selves' in 'Campsite'? What is the poet's attitude throughout the poem?

(b) Compare the mood and message of this poem with Margaret Atwood's poem.

15 (a) Compare and contrast 'Poem for My Sister' by Liz Lochhead (page 94) and 'Football after School' by Patricia McCarthy (page 95). Which poem do you prefer and why? *or*
   (b) Choose any two poems about children or childhood, and give your response to the subject matter, mood and style of writing.

16 'Brothers', page 90. Write briefly about the story told in this poem and then look closely at the language used, picking out anything that you find unusual or interesting. Try writing a section in simple prose and comment on the difference between your rendering and the original.

17 'La Belle Dame sans Merci', page 20. Write about this poem and your response to it. Pick out interesting or difficult lines for comment. What is the atmosphere of the poem and how does Keats create it?

Note: 'The beautiful woman without pity' is the meaning of the title. To understand who is speaking, take careful note of the speech marks.

18 'Shall I Compare Thee …?', page 81.
   (a) What is this sonnet about? Pick out and discuss the images. Do you think the subject matter is outdated?
   (b) Traditionally, sonnets are fourteen lines long with a break or turning point in the subject matter. Can you find any change of emphasis in this sonnet?
   (c) Note down the rhyming scheme and the metre (see *Focus*, pages 135–40). Compare the form of this sonnet with 'The Rose' on page 84.
   (d) Try to write a few lines in iambic pentameters (see *Focus*, page 139). When you have mastered the rhythm, write some rhyming couplets in the same metre or rhythm.
   Note: 'The Rose' is based on the Petrarchan sonnet which came from Italy in the early sixteenth century. Shakespeare, and others, adapted this original form.

19 Make up your own question on one or more of the poems for yourself or for a friend, using ideas from the *Focus* section, pages 135–40.

20 Write a poem in free verse about an important or interesting event in your life. Which section of this anthology would you put your poem in, and why?

INDEX OF FIRST LINES

ACKNOWLEDGEMENTS

The author and publishers would like to thank the following for permission to reproduce copyright material.

p.2 'The Man in the Bowler Hat' by A.S.J. Tessimond from *The Collected Poems of A.S.J. Tessimond* with translations from Jacques Prévert edited by Hubert Nicholson (White Knights Press, 1985) reprinted by permission of the University of Reading; p.3 'Childhood' by Frances Cornford from her *Collected Poems* (1954) reprinted by permission of the Estate of Frances Cornford and the publishers, Hutchinson; p.4 'What happened to the Elephant?' by Sujata Bhatt from *Monkey Shadows* (1988) reprinted by permission of Carcanet Press Ltd; p.5 'Children's Song' by R.S. Thomas from *Penguin Modern Poets* (1962) reprinted by permission of R.S. Thomas; p.6 'Nativity Play' by Tilla Brading reprinted by permission of Tilla Brading; p.7 'A Far Cry from Africa' by Derek Walcott from *Collected Poems* (1948–1984) reprinted by permission of Faber & Faber Ltd; p.8 'The Centre of the Universe' by Paul Durcan reprinted by permission of The Blackstaff Press; p.10 'Telephone Conversation' by Wole Soyinka from *Reflections: Nigerian Prose Verse de Frances Ademola* reprinted by permission of the African Universities Press; p.11 'Campsite: Maentwrog' by U.A. Fanthorpe from *Side Effects* (1978) reprinted by permission of Peterloo Poets; p.12 'At Least a Hundred Words' by Hugo Williams from *Selected Poems* (1989) reprinted by permission of Oxford University Press; p.13 'One' by James Berry from *When I Dance* (1988) © James Berry (first published by Hamish Hamilton Children's Books) reprinted by permission of Penguin Books Ltd; p.14 'Childhood of a Voice' by Martin Carter from *Selected Poems* (Demerara Publications 1968) reprinted by permission of Martin Carter; p.16 'Sheltered Garden' by H.D. from *Beneath the Wide Heaven* (1984) reprinted by permission of Carcanet Press Ltd; p.17 'The Student' by Derek Power reprinted by permission of Derek Power; p.18 'Bogyman' and p.19 'Crab' by Fleur Adcock from *Selected Poems* (1983) reprinted by permission of Oxford University Press; p.22 'Balloons' by Sylvia Plath from *Ariel* reprinted by permission of Faber & Faber Ltd; p.23 'Under the Stairs' from *A Store of Candles* (1986) reprinted with kind permission of Frank Ormsby and The Gallery Press; p.24 'Children Imagining a Hospital' by U.A. Fanthorpe from *Neck Verse* (1992) reprinted by permission of Peterloo Poets; p.26 'The Projectionist's Nightmare' by Brian Patten from *Notes to the Hurrying Man* (1969) reprinted by permission of Allen and Unwin, an imprint of HarperCollins Publishers Ltd; p.26 'Writing a Letter' and p.39 'Six Schoolgirls' by Norman MacCaig from *Collected Poems* reprinted by permission of Chatto & Windus; p.27 'Essential Beauty' by Philip Larkin from *The Whitsun Weddings* reprinted by permission of Faber & Faber Ltd; p.28 'This Poem ...' by Elma Mitchell from *New Poems* (1987) reprinted by permission of Peterloo Poets; p.28 'Sadness as Billy's Leeks Fail to Win a Posthumous Prize' by Linda France from *Headlines in Verse Poetry Now Series* (1993) reprinted by permission of Linda France; p.30 'In the Desert Knowing Nothing' by Helen Dunmore from *Recovering a Body* (1994) reprinted by permission of Bloodaxe Books Ltd; p.31 'The Film of God' and p.57 'The White Tiger' by R.S. Thomas from *Frequencies* reprinted by permission of R.S. Thomas; p.33 'Pavement Artist' by Derek Power reprinted by permission of Derek Power; p.34 'Engineers' Corner' by Wendy Cope from *Making Cocoa for Kingsley*

Amis reprinted by permission of Faber & Faber Ltd; p.37 'Snapshotland' by Sylvia Kantaris from *The Sea at the Door* reprinted by permission of Sylvia Kantaris; p.38 'Background Material' by Tony Harrison from *Selected Poems* (Penguin 1989) reprinted by permission of Tony Harrison; p.40 'The Old Story' by Patricia McCarthy from *A Second Skin* reprinted by permission of Peterloo Poets; p.41 'My Family' by Paul D. Wapshott from *The Poetry of War* reprinted by permission of Paul D. Wapshott; p.42 'Family Portraits' by Angela Costen reprinted by permission of Angela Costen; p.44 'Manifesto on *Ars Poetica*' by Frank Chipasula reprinted by permission of Frank Chipasula; p.46 'Not My Best Side' by U.A. Fanthorpe from *Side Effects* (1978) reprinted by permission of Peterloo Poets; p.48 'TV' by Iain Crichton Smith from *The Village and Other Poems* reprinted by permission of Carcanet Press Ltd; p.50 'Song of the Battery Hen' by Edwin Brock from *Five Ways to Kill a Man* reprinted by permission of Enitharmon Press; p.51 'Neighbours' by Gillian Clarke from *Letting in the Rumour* (1989) reprinted by permission of Carcanet Press Ltd; p.54 'The Magpie's Son' by Sheila Glen Bishop reprinted by permission of Sheila Glen Bishop; p.56 'Special Green' by Robert Etty reprinted by permission of Robert Etty; p.59 'Distance Collapsed in Rubble' by Anna Akhmatova, translated by Richard McKane, from *Selected Poems by Anna Akhmatova* (1989) reprinted by permission of Bloodaxe Books Ltd; p.60 'Permafrost' by Helen Dunmore from *Short Days, Long Nights: New and Selected Poems* (1991) reprinted by permission of Bloodaxe Books Ltd; p.61 'Augury' by Seamus Heaney from *Wintering Out* reprinted by permission of Faber & Faber Ltd; p.63 'Pigeons' by Patricia Beer from *Collected Poems* (1988) reprinted by permission of Carcanet Press Ltd; p.63 'Snow' by Louis MacNeice from *The Collected Poems of Louis MacNeice* edited by E.R. Dobbs and reprinted by permission of Faber & Faber Ltd; p.70 'A Holiday' by Margaret Atwood from *Interlunar* © Margaret Atwood 1984, reprinted by permission of Oxford University Press, Canada; p.71 'Runaway' by Linda France from *Red* (1992) reprinted by permission of Bloodaxe Books Ltd; p.72 'Kankaria Lake' by Sujata Bhatt reprinted by permission of Carcanet Press Ltd; p.76 'I'm Really Very Fond' and 'Walker' by Alice Walker from *Horses Make a Landscape Look More Beautiful* (first published in Great Britain by The Women's Press Ltd (1985) 34 Great Sutton Street, London EC1V 0DX) reprinted by permission of David Higham Associates; p.79 'One Flesh' by Elizabeth Jennings from *Collected Poems* (1986) published by Carcanet Press Ltd; p.80 'Anniversaries' by Andrew Motion from *Dangerous Play* (Penguin) reprinted by permission of the Peters, Fraser & Dunlop Group Ltd; p.82 'People Etcetera' by Elma Mitchell from *New Poems* (1987) reprinted by permission of Peterloo Poets; p.83 'A Blade of Grass' by Brian Patten from *Love Poems* reprinted by permission of HarperCollins Publishers Ltd; p.84 'In Our Tenth Year' by Simon Armitage from *Kid* reprinted by permission of Faber & Faber Ltd; p.84 'The Rose' by Peter Dale reprinted by permission of Peter Dale and Agenda/Carcanet Press Ltd; p.85 'Flying Saucer' by John Hawkhead reprinted by permission of John Hawkhead; p.86 'Sonnet' by Edna St Vincent Millay from *Collected Poems*, HarperCollins (copyright 1917, 1945 by Edna St Vincent Millay) reprinted by permission of Elizabeth Barnett, literary executor; p.87 'You Were Saying' by Patricia and John Hawkhead reprinted by permission of Patricia and John Hawkhead; p.89 'Follower' by Seamus Heaney from *Death of a Naturalist* reprinted by permission of Faber & Faber Ltd; p.91 'Registers' by

Michael Laskey from *Thinking of Happiness* reprinted by permission of Peterloo Poets; p.92 'The Gift' by Chris Banks reprinted by permission of Chris Banks; p.93 'Laundrette' and p.94 'Poem for My Sister' by Liz Lochhead from *Dreaming Frankenstein* reprinted by permission of Polygon; p.95 'Football after School' by Patricia McCarthy from *A Second Skin* reprinted by permission of Peterloo Poets; p.98 'Lament' by Wilfred Gibson from *Collected Poems* (1926) reprinted by permission of Macmillan General Books; p.99 'For a Dead African' by John Nangoza Jebe from *Poets to the People* edited by Barry Feinberg, published by George Allen & Unwin and reprinted by permission of HarperCollins; p.99 'Suicide in the Trenches' and p.109 'The General' by Siegfried Sassoon reprinted by permission of George Sassoon; p.101 'Flying the Flag in Bosnia' by Derek Power reprinted by permission of Derek Power; p.102 'Two Fusiliers' by Robert Graves reprinted by permission of A.P. Watt Ltd on behalf of The Trustees of the Robert Graves Copyright Trust; p.103 'Dulce et Decorum Est' by Wilfred Owen from *The Poems of Wilfred Owen* edited by Jon Stallworthy, published by The Hogarth Press and reprinted by permission of Random House UK Ltd; p.104 'Rhodesia' by Peter Moulding reprinted by permission of Peter Moulding; p.105 'Casualty – Mental Ward' by Vernon Scannell from *The Poetry of War* edited by Simon Fuller and reprinted by permission of Vernon Scannell; p.107 'MCMXIV' by Philip Larkin from *The Whitsun Weddings* reprinted by permission of Faber & Faber Ltd; p.108 'A Motorbike' by Ted Hughes from *Moortown* reprinted by permission of Faber & Faber Ltd; p.110 '*from* Bayonet Training' by Vernon Scannell from *The Poetry of War* edited by Simon Fuller and reprinted by permission of Vernon Scannell; p.111 'Incubator' by Iain Crichton Smith from *The Village and Other Poems* (1989) reprinted by permission of Carcanet Press Ltd; p.113 'Children in Wartime' by Isobel Thrilling from *The Poetry of War* (BBC/Longman) reprinted by permission of Isobel Thrilling; p.115 'Waiting for Thelma's Laughter' by Grace Nichols from *The Fat Black Woman's Poems* reprinted by kind permission of the publishers, Virago Press; p.116 'deconstruction ...' by Tilla Brading reprinted by permission of Tilla Brading; p.117 'The Bicycle Ride' by Selima Hill from *Saying Hello at the Station* (Chatto & Windus 1984) reprinted by permission of Selima Hill; p.120 'Thoughts After Visiting Westminster City Council's Archives' by Kay Hargreaves reprinted by permission of Kay Hargreaves; p.121 'Tich Miller' by Wendy Cope from *Making Cocoa for Kingsley Amis* reprinted by permission of Faber & Faber Ltd; p.122 'You Will Forget' by Chenjerai Hove from 'The Red Hills of Home' in the *Heinemann Book of African Poetry in English* reprinted by permission of The Mambo Press; p.124 'People' by Charlotte Zolotow from *All that Sunlight* (1967) reprinted by permission of Harper & Row Publishers Ltd.

Every effort has been made to reach copyright holders; the publishers would like to hear from anyone whose rights they have unknowingly infringed.